TOM JONES: AN EXTRAORDINARY LIFE

The owner of one of the most recognizable faces – not to mention voices – in the entertainment business, Sir Tom Jones is the definition of a national treasure. It has been over fifty years since Jones's breakthrough single 'It's Not Unusual' reached Number One in the UK, but success wasn't always assured for the Welsh entertainer. Having overcome childhood tuberculosis, Tom Jones married his teenage girlfriend at the age of sixteen. With a young family to support, it seemed far more likely that a career as a vacuum salesman was beckoning. Bestselling biographer Gwen Russell charts Jones's journey from young, unsigned local singer to one of Britain's best-loved entertainers.

Tom Jones: An Extraordinary Life

by

Gwen Russell

Magna Large Print Books
Long Preston, North Yorkshire,
BD23 4ND, England.

British Library Cataloguing in Publication Data.

A catalogue record of this book is
available from the British Library

ISBN   978-0-7505-4522-8

First published in Great Britain by John Blake Publishing Ltd in 2009

Text copyright © Gwen Russell 2015

Cover illustration © Featureflash Photo Agency/Shutterstock.com by arrangement with Shutterstock.com

The right of Gwen Russell to be identified as the author of this work has been asserted by her in accordance with the Copyright, Designs and Patents Act, 1988

Published in Large Print 2018 by arrangement with
John Blake Publishing Ltd.

Magna Large Print is an imprint of Library Magna Books Ltd.

Printed and bound in Great Britain by
T.J. (International) Ltd., Cornwall, PL28 8RW

CONTENTS

INTRODUCTION

The date was 9 February 1998, and the crowd was going wild. Robbie Williams, the man the *Sun* called the biggest pop phenomenon in Britain since The Beatles, had taken to the stage at the annual Brit awards, where he had the audience in the palm of his hand. The crowd, especially the girls, adored him, and as he launched into a rendition of 'You Can Keep Your Hat On', the screaming reached a crescendo. Suddenly the audience's attention turned elsewhere. Another voice had started to sing, one of the most powerful voices to be heard in pop music over the last 40 years. It was that of Tom Jones.

Tom had, quite simply, done it again. Thirty-five years older than Robbie, he had quite effortlessly upstaged him by the sheer impact of his singing. Not that Robbie was going down without a fight, of course: he pushed his own singing to the limits, bound himself into contortions, and engaged with the audience as never before. It was a bravura performance – and one that was tempted out of him by Tom. And it is a testament to Tom's charm and charisma that, after the Brits, the two men, far from acting as rivals, became firm friends.

CHAPTER 1

44 LAURA STREET
PONTYPRIDD

Can there be a more popular entertainer than the Welsh singer Tom Jones? One of the most enduring celebrities of our day, he first appeared on the scene in the early 1960s and actually started his career as a teen idol, but swiftly changed tack to become the more sophisticated singer he is today. It's not just his sheer raw talent and voice that hold such appeal, however. Throughout his life he has also been a sex symbol, to the extent that although he was already in his sixties when he received his knighthood, clever headline writers knew his fans would love an ever-appropriate reference to one of his biggest hits, greeting him with headlines such as 'Arise, Sir Sex Bomb'. At one stage he was almost as famous for the lingerie shop's worth of knickers that was thrown on to his stage every night as he was for his singing, but still 'Tom the Voice' shone through. After more than forty years in the business, he still shows no signs of letting up, continuing to perform in concert and live the high life, something he does to great aplomb.

It's all a very long way from his origins in Pontypridd, the pride of the Rhonda in the valleys of South Wales. While many showbusiness stars like to turn roots that are solidly middle class into something a little bit more exciting, Tom is the real deal. He comes from an achingly poor background, with a father who spent his life working down the pits – something Tom was able to rescue him from the moment he had the means – and he left school with little prospects, which led to some very dead-end jobs. No one in the family was in showbusiness so there was no way they could possibly have predicted what lay in store for young Tom. Nor was he a trained singer: early on the family realised it had a boy with a mighty fine voice on its hands, but there was no question of them being able to do anything about it with a view to Tom singing professionally. For a start, there wasn't the money and even if there had been, it wasn't the sort of thing his family would have dreamt of, so alien was the concept of a son in the world of showbusiness. But that's the way it turned out, with Tom leading a life of international fame and stardom, culminating in the ultimate accolade of a knighthood.

Way back in the beginning, it was all so very different. On 7 June 1940 Thomas Jones Woodward was born to Thomas Woodward, a miner, and housewife Freda Woodward, née Jones. Until Tom was four, they lived in 57 Kingsland Terrace in Treforest, near Pontypridd, when they moved to 44 Laura Street, which was where he grew up. His parents were delighted at their new arrival and right from the start, he was a very attractive little boy, as his mother remembered: 'Oh, he was such a pretty little boy,' she said. 'It used to frighten me sometimes, thinking somebody might want to take him away.' Indeed, when Tom was two and a half and the family was on holiday on Barry Island, he did go missing for over an hour before his frantic mother finally found him. 'I took him by the hand and was walking back when a woman we passed said, "Oh look, there's little Tommy Woodward, 44 Laura Street, Pontypridd." "How do you know that?" I asked her, astonished. "Well," she said, "I caught hold of him, and he told me his name and address very plainly, but he wouldn't stay with me."'

They were a musical family and from very early on, Tom was exposed to performing. On Saturday nights his parents would sing at the Wood Road Non-Political Club, where his Uncle George booked the acts. Tom was encouraged to sing everywhere else, too. At chapel he sang the Lord's Prayer and 'Barbara Allen' at Treforest Secondary Modern School. From a very early age he had an exceptionally powerful voice: during choir practice renditions of 'Men of Harlech' sometimes had to be abandoned as he out-rumbled everyone else. Of course, the musical traditions of Wales are very strong, which encouraged him greatly, something of which he was well aware. 'In Wales there are choirs, especially male-voice choirs, which a lot of my cousins were in,' he recalled. 'A Welsh tenor will have a full Welsh voice, even though he's singing high, full-blown window shattering material. Maybe speaking Welsh lends itself, the accent ... maybe part of it is the cheapest way of making music is to sing. You don't need to buy an instrument.' Even so, he was a precocious little boy. 'When I was four I used to stand on a box in the corner of the grocer's while my mother was doing the shopping and sing to the customers and collect the pennies,' he once revealed.

Right from the start his mother Freda knew she had an entertainer on her hands. From a very young age Tom's voice was remarkable and he always knew what he wanted to do. He developed a habit of jumping up on to the windowsill, pulling the curtains across and demanding his mother joined in. Decades later, he mused: 'She'd say, "Look, I'm busy, I'm trying to clean the house." And I would say, "No, I want you to introduce me." Anyway, she'd do it and I'd throw back the curtains and jump out. Even though there was nobody there but my mother.' Sometimes, though, he had an audience of two when his sister Sheila was persuaded to watch.

But it was a tough life and the family was typical of the area and of the time. 'When my father was down the mine, he was a hard-working, hard-drinking man,' Tom later recalled. 'He used to like his cards and a flutter on the horses. He used to go out on the booze on Saturdays and I looked up to him. He put my mother in her place and they used to fight, but it was a healthy upbringing.' At an early age Tom's view of marriage was formed: the man would go out and bring home the bacon and the woman would cook it; the man would also rule the roost. It was how his later life was to pan out. But certainly he idolised his father. 'I always thought what a good physique he had and I wanted to be like him,' he remembered. 'When I was little, I yearned to be a man, to be the best I could. I have a memory of being a small boy, hearing a noise in the night and my father getting up to see what it was. I remember thinking, "When I grow up, will I be as brave as that?"'

Just before he entered his teens, two things happened that had a profound bearing on his future. For a start, aged just eleven, he met a local Catholic girl (also eleven) when she was playing marbles close to where he lived. Her name was Melinda Trenchard, although she was more commonly known as Linda and the two hit it off immediately. 'I went to a Protestant school so we didn't mix that much but I always liked those Catholic girls because they wore little gold earrings,' he recalled. 'Very sexy. So I saw her playing marbles – and she had great legs.'

Linda was indeed an attractive girl. 'She was a very, very pretty girl and popular,' says Jean Thomas, one of Tom's cousins on his mother's side. 'She was a catch, stunning with short, blonde hair and she had what they called a "DA" [duck's arse], a little tuft at the back of her neck. She was also very fashion conscious and had the first of everything. I remember clutch bags; she was one of the first to have a clutch bag. They knew one another in school. I think she was just in a class lower and I think she was a bit cleverer than Tom and I. I always remember she was in the A classes. She also liked fashion and boys, as girls do.'

Shortly after they met, however, Tom was diagnosed with tuberculosis, which caused him to be bedridden for nearly two years. Never exactly an academic child – he was actually found to be dyslexic in later life – he could not have been too upset at the news that he would be off school as he recovered in bed. But no one could foresee the influence this period at home was to have on his later life. Tom spent a year listening to the radio where, for the first time, he began to listen to American music – Blues, Rhythm and Blues, Rock'n'Roll – and he loved it. 'The exaggeration,' he said. 'The drama. It's like Gospel as opposed to the Church of England.'

Nonetheless, the family was very worried. For some time Tom was extremely ill, so much so that there were concerns that he wouldn't pull through. He was a tough little boy, though, fighting against his illness and determined to get better as soon as he could. The adult Tom never complains about those days: rather, he prefers to remember the way they opened up the musical world to him. Had he but known it, he was already learning his trade and this period was a crucial one in his development. Later, when he started to make records, many people assumed he was a black singer and the way he made his American breakthrough was by being featured on radio stations that played black music. According to him this was something that just happened: 'I was listening to the BBC radio in the late forties, early fifties, when I was a kid and anytime a Gospel or Blues song would come on, I would think: "What is that?" It was rubbing off on me. I didn't know why, I just liked it. In school I sang the Lord's Prayer, and my teacher said to me, "Why are you singing this like a Negro spiritual?" I didn't know what the term was, I was very young – seven, eight – it was very natural for me to do it.

'What attracted me to Rock'n'Roll was the sound. I toured with Count Basie once and I asked him what he thought of it, and he said, "What they've done, which we used to do, is to concentrate on the rhythm section, get that rhythm section hot. When Jerry Lee Lewis pounds out and the rhythm section kicks in with him, you can balance it because you don't have all those other instruments to worry about." When I heard Jerry Lee's "Whole Lotta Shakin' Goin' On", the piano starts like this...' [Tom started to jab an imaginary keyboard as he spoke] 'and Sam Phillips [the owner of Sun Records] had a slap-back echo because he didn't have an echo chamber so he created a tape delay. He'd have two tapes running, with one a little stronger than the other. It's only a simple thing that Jerry Lee is playing but because of that slap-back things hadn't sounded like that before.'

But this was all to come and the other effect of the months in bed was that Tom formed an exceptionally close bond with his mother Freda. A generous man, who looked after all his family once he had become rich, it was his mother to whom he felt particularly close and he never forgot how she had looked after him when he was so ill. That determination to get well again must surely have had a hand in shaping his character for he was by no means an overnight success: for years he was forced to slog before he finally made his break-through and despite moments of despair, he never gave up. His longevity in such a fickle business can also be attributed to a determination to keep going, for there were to be some major blips in his career, when it must have seemed as if it might indeed be all over. But no matter what frustrations there must have been, he never gave up.

Tom regained his health and, aged twelve, he returned to school. But he took to academia no more than he ever had done, instead spending his time chasing girls and playing truant. His was a rough childhood and it toughened him up. Sometimes he got into trouble, although he says his mother's impeccable house often saved him. 'When the officials came to see my mother,' he explained, 'with the brass nicely polished in the front room, picture of granddad with his medals on, they went away sayin', "No ruffian could live here!"' Sometimes he got into fights, which was to bring on an obsession with his nose that would last for decades. 'That's why I hate my horrible nose – it's been worked over, bent sideways and patched up more than any other part of me,' he once said. 'And always hit by a head – we liked to keep our hands nice and smooth, like!' In fact, his nose was one of the first things about him to change once he became famous: at the earliest possible opportunity he had it whittled down.

In later years, Tom played down this aspect of his life, although he was always perfectly honest about what had gone on. When he first became famous quite a bit was made of his wild youth, something he gradually began to edge away from. 'People say to me from time to time, "Oh yes, you used to get involved in punch-ups years ago, didn't you?"' he said in 1969. 'I can't disagree with that. Now I've grown up, I'll be twenty-nine in June. So have all the boys I used to hang about with when we were tearaways. They're quiet now. Married. They don't fight any more.' In the background, though, there was always the singing. Freda later said that she sensed her son would go far. Asked what quality it was that she considered had taken Tom to the top, she replied, 'Determination. One day he came and said to me, "Mum, the day will come when I will prove myself." He was about fifteen then, but I knew it had been in his mind long before; it was the one thing he wanted and he stuck at it.'

Tom left school at sixteen with no qualifications and no clear idea about what he wanted to do. As a boy, school had not been important to him although in later life he regretted not taking his studies more seriously. 'I sometimes wish I had paid more attention in school,' he once confessed. 'I used to listen to Radio Luxembourg under the bedcovers at night rather than do my homework. I have made up for it since. There's nothing like travel to finish off an education. There are very few countries I have not been to, and I am credited for being one of the first white performers to insist on singing to mixed audiences in South Africa.'

One thing was clear back then: he was going to have to marry Linda, who was also sixteen, not least because she was pregnant – in actual fact the couple had just turned seventeen when the wedding took place. But Tom assumed his responsibilities cheerfully: for some years now the two had been sweethearts and the match was regarded favourably by the family. 'They are so easy in each other's company, they are pals,' said Linda's mother, Jean. 'There's a spark. I think they were going with each other since about thirteen. She loves him and he loves her that's for definite. I have seen them quite a few times together, even when they were young. They used to go drinking. I can see them now smooching; I remember them getting married. Tom was seventeen in the June, and she was seventeen the following February, just a bit younger. They got married and my Gran always said, "They were made for each other." There's definitely something there. I have been in their company. You can tell how much they love one another.'

A great deal has been written about the unusual nature of Tom and Linda's marriage, in that while he turned out to have a bit of an eye for the ladies, in later years Linda became extremely reclusive. But there has never been any question of divorce. The reason is that the marriage has incredibly strong roots dating back to their friendship as children, which turned into courtship, which ultimately became a bond that goes far deeper than many other, more superficial unions. There are very few people in Tom's life that knew him before he was famous and know exactly what his background and childhood was like, but one of them is Linda. When they met they weren't even in their teens and all this has provided the basis of an enduring partnership.

It has been a love match for both of them, but even in the very earliest days Tom was already showing himself to be a man's man. Chatting to his father on his way back from the Pontypridd Register Office, his father said, 'Don't you think you should be walking with your bride?' But that early marriage was to be the making of Tom in that it made him accept his responsibilities. 'It gave me more drive, more determination,' he later said. 'I had my own family, there was a bigger need in me now to succeed.' But doing what? For the young Tom there was no obvious career path to follow and nothing that he clearly wanted to do above all else. And so he held down a variety of jobs that led nowhere: as a builder's mate, a paper miller, a glove cutter and a door-to-door salesman. Money was extremely tight: the new family lived with Linda's parents in Cliff Terrace with, at that time, not much immediate chance of getting a home of their own.

'I had married at seventeen – Linda was my childhood sweetheart – and I was about to be a father,' Tom recalled on a separate occasion when he had finally moved to the States permanently. 'I had responsibilities and no money. I remember phoning the hospital to find out if Linda had had our baby yet. They told me we had a son, Mark. The phone box I called from is outside in my Bel Air garden now. I managed to acquire the old Button A, Button B four-penny phone kiosk from the end of my street in South Wales.

'When I was eighteen, if you had dialled Ponty-pridd 3667, the chances were you would have got me in that box, which used to stand in Laura Street. That was my first phone, my first office. I courted girls from it, my family began in it (not literally, mind you) and it's as much a part of my life as my first gold record. I am a sentimentalist at heart and when I heard the heartless GPO was going to tear it down and replace it with some newfangled device, I had a friend in Wales make a few calls for me. It now stands beside the pool

21

at my home. Of course, it wasn't my exclusive line. We lived in a mining community and in those days miners couldn't afford phones. Sometimes there would be a long queue of people waiting to use it.'

The Tom of those days was a very different person from the man of today. Not only was he a small town boy who knew nothing of the wider world, but he was a creature very much of that particular time. It was the late 1950s, a world that now seems so far removed from our own that it could have been hundreds of years ago rather than mere decades. 'When I was eighteen, I suppose I was a Teddy Boy – that was my era, only a few years before National Service was abolished in 1960,' he said. 'It was all Elvis, Jerry Lee Lewis, Carl Perkins, Little Richard, Fats Domino, our own Tommy Steele, Marty Wilde, even Terry Dene. I wish I'd known I was going to join their ranks because I worried a lot.'

Tom spent his spare time and money in the pubs and clubs of Pontypridd absorbing the new types of music that were coming over from the States. While this was something he did purely for pleasure, it was to have a huge effect on his career. 'We didn't have rock bands then because it was a new music,' he said. 'So I didn't particularly like going to those big dance halls with those live dance bands because they were not playing Rock'n'Roll music. So we would have to wait until the interval when the band took a break, then they would play Rock'n'Roll records, and that was the best part of the night for me, which was only like a fifteen-minute thing, you know, while the band had a break. So then you would hear these American rock records. But then we had our own dance halls in Pontypridd. There was one called The Ranch, which used to be these old buildings that were built there during the War to house American troops, and they were still standing in the fifties. So there was one up in Ponty called The Ranch, and there was one in Rhydfelin called The Legion, which I think was the British Legion.

'Those dance halls, they would only play records, which was perfect. I loved that because you were getting American Rock'n'Roll music first hand. You know the real deal as opposed to some old dance band trying to play it. I mean, it wasn't working, you know, just not for us it wasn't anyway.' What this came to mean was that when the right time came, Tom would be able to sing Rock'n'Roll. It was not the style that was going to make him famous, but it did make an impression on the locals who heard him, which helped to build up his reputation before he made it big.

His love of music was growing. Linda constantly encouraged him to work in the clubs. He might have been getting nowhere in the day job, but by night he was doing what he loved best: singing. There was some experimentation with guitar playing and on the drums, but over and again he returned to the instrument for which he had the most talent: his voice. For the first time, he began to think that that was where the future might lie: as a professional singer. 'I went to a singing teacher in Wales, thinking that if I was going to become a professional singer I should do the job properly,' he related. 'She advised me not to attempt to have my voice trained. She said, "You sing naturally, which is right for pop music, because pop music is an informal type of expression. Training would take away your spontaneity. Musically speaking, some of your notes are wrong but they are part of your individual style." She was pleased with the way I "opened up" [projected his voice instead of keeping a lot of notes in his head, which is the fault of many untrained singers]. However, I needed to have my breathing put right, which she did for me.'

The teacher in question could not have been more right. While there are other powerful and good-looking singers around, Tom's inimitable style, set him apart from the competition. It was, and is unique, and it's easy to see how formal training might have spoiled that. But it's equally clear that Tom, untrained or not, was massively talented musically, something that became apparent when he talked about his art. Music was to be his life. 'Although I do not read music, I do have a good ear and memory,' he once said. 'All I need is for somebody to play the melody of a new song once, then by reading the words I can go straight into a recording session. Incidentally, my voice never broke as a boy. It just got steadily deeper. My range is to top C, which I can read in the keys I sing, but I do not know my bottom note.'

When his son Mark was a toddler, Tom decided to throw in his day job and, once and for all, go for a singing career. But it was a very big risk. For a start, Linda had to go out to work, something

Tom hated. As a traditional Welshman, he felt that it should be the man who provides. But if he was to get anywhere, he had to accept it. If he carried on working during the day, it was not going to be possible to put in the hours needed to build a singing career and so, with a certain amount of bravery, he took the decision that his life lay elsewhere. At first he performed alone in working men's clubs, where his act was hugely popular, while his first actual paid performance was at the Wood Road Non-Political Club in Treforest in 1958. He earned £1 for playing two sets of three songs each.

It was a hard slog, and one that was ultimately going to take six years to achieve, although there was the odd hint that bigger things were to come. On one occasion, Tom inadvertently managed to upstage a singer called Danny Williams: 'One night after I'd been working the clubs in South Wales, I ended up having a few drinks at a Cardiff nightclub,' he recalled. 'Danny wasn't going too well. He had a quiet voice, and people kept drinking and talking, so he was annoyed. When he got to his last number, he said, "Gentlemen, you can join in and sing this one if you want to." I'd had a few drinks, so I started to sing. Everybody in the audience stopped, including Danny Williams. I had taken over. I left the bar and we teamed up for "Moon River" – and brought the house down.'

Tom was also learning his trade. While his voice may not have needed training, the rest of him certainly did, and it was in these rough pubs and clubs that he began to discover exactly how to deal with an audience. Of course there was a

25

certain amount of banter involved, just as there is today, but he had to learn how to handle aggressive punters and deal with heckling. He also needed to know how to charm his listeners and win them over with song. This was the musical equivalent of a stand-up comedian touring the rough crowds in the provinces before coming out with a smooth patter on TV to more sophisticated audiences. It gave him a chance to learn the tricks of the trade before the public spotlight fell on him and it was a training that was to stand him in very good stead.

Tom was, of course, also in the right place at the right time, in terms of this being the late fifties and early sixties, something he himself was only too happy to agree with. The seismic changes in society that were beginning to happen were hugely beneficial to people like him and in the 1960s there was nothing more fashionable than a working-class boy made good. Opportunities were opening up that wouldn't have existed before, society was becoming more fluid and old certainties changing. A generation previously, Tom might well have had a life identical to his father's, one that would very soon have ruined his remarkable voice. 'I did once think that I would be a miner like Dad,' he said in an interview. 'It's a Welsh tradition, or it was when I was eighteen, that a lad would follow his family down the pits. My dad, Tom Senior, spent his life, until I could afford to get him out, digging coal and he paid the ultimate price that many miners do: his lungs were affected.'

It was a harsh life, although courtesy of their

generous son, Tom's parents were to end their days in great luxury. But it was his good fortune to be part of a generation that was opening up to new thoughts and ideas, refusing to be hidebound by the traditions of the past. For all the worries and uncertainty he experienced until his career got going, it was a glorious time to be young and full of hope and ambition. The world was there for the taking, and he went out and grabbed every opportunity he could find. 'At eighteen, everyone wishes that something is going to happen to them that is going to change their life drastically,' he said. 'It did happen for me. I was part of an era that changed everything – fashion, music, films, even our way of thinking and our morals.'

It was indeed. And another aspect of Tom's character that stood him in very good stead was that when he met the right people, he was willing to allow himself to be guided. He was sensible enough to realise that while he might have the voice, others had business sense and the ability to plan ahead. In the early days he changed direction several times and again, his apprenticeship playing in rural Wales allowed him to find what he was capable of doing best. At that stage it didn't matter if he made mistakes because he was still playing to a very restricted audience who were not going to hold it against him. Of course, at the time Tommy Woodward had no idea he was destined to become one of the biggest international stars of his generation. Back then it seemed the best he could hope for was to make a bit of money by singing, just enough to keep his family on, without having

27

to become a miner himself. And he was certainly becoming noticed locally. His voice was so powerful that he could hardly hide himself in the shadows: once he started singing, people really sat up and took notice.

While Tom was to acquire fame later on as a solo singer, he had his first big break when he joined a band. In fact, it was the band that approached him. A Beat outfit named, coincidentally, Tommy Scott and the Senators, had just lost their lead singer (Tommy Redman), who had decided to go off in a different direction and sing ballads. Fortunately, one of the band members knew Tom. Desperate to replace their lead singer, in 1963 he decided to approach him to join the band. What happened next is one of those make-or-break moments that have shaped so many careers without the person at the centre of it all realising quite what a momentous event was about to take place. When Tommy Redman failed to show up one night, the bandleader – Vernon Hopkins – asked Tom if he would go on stage. His first reaction was incredulity, for it was Friday night, traditionally the night the local boys went out with their girlfriends and, worse still, the venue was the YMCA! This was not only uncool but no alcohol was allowed and then, as now, he enjoyed a drink. But Vernon needed someone, and fast! He promised Tom that if he agreed to appear, he would make sure a crate of beer was smuggled into the premises. Rather reluctantly, he consented to play for one night, but one night was all it took. The evening was a resounding success and, buoyed up by the audience's reaction,

Tom signed up with the band. It would be a while yet before he hit the big time, but Tommy Woodward was on his way.

CHAPTER 2

TIGER TOM, THE TWISTING VOCALIST

Things were getting serious. Tom had now made the decision to pursue a career in music in earnest, and it was a far from straightforward road that lay ahead. It was also financially precarious. The couple still had no money and now, on Tom's side at least, no fixed income, and what he did earn wouldn't have taken them far. Singing in the pubs and clubs of Wales was not a well-paid occupation, but by now he was determined to make a go of it, and he took to his new career with gusto.

He also, for pretty much the only time in his entire career, managed to persuade Linda to come along to watch him perform. Much has been made of the fact that Tom's wife doesn't attend his concerts because she doesn't like the way other women respond to him (and who can blame her?). But there is another element in her reticence, too: Tom's act is pretty highly charged, not simply because of his cavorting, but also the sheer scale and range of his voice and Linda was constantly anxious that something would go wrong. In the event, her presence was not a great success. 'In the end, she got so bloody drunk that I had to go into the ladies' room to get her out once the whole thing was over,' said a wry Tom. 'She'd bloody collapsed in there because she'd got too excited. That's the way she's always felt. If I go for a high note, she's worried I'm not going to make it.' And that, as far as Linda attending Tom's concerts was concerned, was that.

Now that he was in a band, changes had to be made. For a start, Tommy Woodward became Tommy Scott and, dressed in black leather, he began to perform with his new friends. At his suggestion, the music was Rock'n'Roll, with the result that the local pub owners would take one look at the leather, the instruments, and offer to pay the band off without them actually playing. But Tom managed to persuade them to think again. 'I said, "Wait a minute,"' he recalled. '"Let's start the show. After a while, if we do three or four tunes and you're bothered by it and people are not digging it, fair enough." So there we were on a Saturday night, and "Pay 'em off!" became, "Do you think we can get an extension if we call the police tonight?" And did we mind if they moved all the tables and chairs so everyone could have a dance? And I said, "By all means." So I introduced Rock'n'Roll to Welsh working men's clubs. They had never had it before.'

He wasn't exaggerating (or at least, not much). Since he was a teenager Tom had been listening to Rock'n'Roll in the dance halls, which meant, in effect, he'd been preparing for the moment when he would play it himself. 'We were being influenced a lot by that kind of music,' he said. 'So then I would incorporate it into, you know, if I got up into a pub. I learned to play guitar because the piano players around couldn't play it. It was a music that they were not used to. So, if you went into a pub in Pontypridd and there was a piano player there, nine times out of ten they wouldn't be playing Rock'n'Roll. So I started – I learned to play the guitar in order to accompany myself. You know, so I used to go to a pub called The Wheatsheaf in Ponty and I'd take the guitar there on a Friday night and a Saturday night, and get up and make my own Rock'n'Roll music.'

It was a rough old time but Tom had the stamina to cope with it. 'They would ring the police station to get the licence extended till midnight, and I would sing for hours with just the odd break for a pint at the bar,' he recalled on another occasion. It wasn't just the odd pint – friends from those days remember he managed to get through about ten or twelve of them without the alcohol having an effect on his performance at all. Indeed, he was to become as well known for being a *bon viveur* as he was for his other excesses, although in time it was champagne, rather than beer, that would become his tipple of choice.

Inch by inch, he was beginning to make his mark, gathering a devoted following in South Wales. He continued to upstage everyone around him: an early gig was in Porthcawl, where the Senators were supporting Billy J Kramer and the Dakotas. They were such a hit with the audience that Kramer had to let them perform a second set to pacify all those present: it was Tom who seemed to be the star of the show rather than anyone else.

31

With that kind of audience reaction, he was bound to come to the attention of the professionals and the first people to realise his potential were Raymond Godfrey and John Glastonbury, also known as Meirion and Byron. The two were songwriters and, on seeing the Senators playing in Caerphilly, they realised that here was a man who had the capacity to make it to the very top. They were just what Tom needed at the time: they had contacts with the music business in London and, until he made his breakthrough in London, the centre of the music industry, he hadn't a hope of achieving fame – and they were able to offer some much-needed guidance.

With a producer called Joe Meek of Telstar Records, Godfrey and Glastonbury helped the Senators to make a demo tape with a view to a major label picking it up, but none of them were particularly interested, and nor did that relationship run smoothly. The band were hoping to release a single called 'Lonely Joe / I Was A Fool', but Meek then refused to release the tapes. It was an extremely frustrating period for all concerned. But Godfrey and Glastonbury did have those all-important London contacts and so it was that Tom was discovered for the first time by Peter Sullivan of Decca Records, who realised that here was a truly impressive singing talent. He was persuaded to move briefly down to London, where, on the recommendation of Decca Records A&R [Artist & Repertoire] man Dick Rowe, he was given a manager: Phil Solomon, described by one person as an 'imperious entrepreneur'. What seemed like a major breakthrough was not to last, however. The two men did not get on and so, with his career still at its earliest stages, Tom returned to Wales.

While he was having that early London adventure and trying to make it as a singer, back in Wales Linda kept the home fires burning, working to support the family. She is remembered as being a vivacious girl in those days, bright and easygoing and very popular. 'She was a beautiful girl,' said Dorothy Woodward, another of Tom's cousins on his father's side. 'Maybe she grew up too quickly. She was very glamorous, right up to date. The short crop hair, the DA. At that time she was quite outgoing. When Tom was in London trying to make his name she worked the evenings with my other sister on Treforest Trading Estate. She was always jolly, quite good fun to be with, chatty.'

Of course, Linda was young and pretty, and all alone while her husband was trying to make the big time in London. What, Tom was once asked, would he have done if the unthinkable happened and Linda had cast her eyes elsewhere? He was incredulous at the very thought. 'My wife cheating on me?' he asked. 'Well, it would never happen. When I first went to London, that was the closest. She used to go out with a girlfriend and fellas would bring her home but that's as far as it went. I've got a lot of friends there, see. I don't think she'd be able to get away with it without being noticed. She never wanted to, as far as I know. I would never question her about it, unless it was brought to my attention.' It never was, of course, as Linda remained an utterly loyal wife, keeping the little family in Wales together.

Meanwhile, Tom slogged on. Here is a taste of what life for him was like in those early days. In 1964 he sang in the White Hart pub. 'I was paid a tenner,' he said, 'which I had to split five ways.' But his life really was changing now, for his reputation was spreading and, while he still hadn't broken through in London circles, people were beginning to talk about this handsome young Welshman with the astonishing voice. He had his own following and fans would follow him around Wales to see him. Sooner or later it was inevitable that he would be discovered and the person who finally did so was fellow Welshman Gordon Mills. A character in himself, he was a former bus conductor who later informed the public that he had the largest collection of orang-utans in the world!

Gordon went to see the Senators at the Top Hat in 1964, a club in Cwmtillery. It took him no time at all to realise quite what a talent was on show there. 'The first few bars were all I needed to hear,' he said. 'They convinced me that here was a voice that could make him the greatest singer in the world.' He lost no time in approaching Tom. This time singer and manager hit it off and Gordon took Tom to London to begin the serious business of getting him known. To do so, he had to make a deal with Godfrey and Glastonbury, who were still his managers. In return for 5 per cent of Tom's future earnings they gave up their role, which unfortunately became the subsequent basis for legal wrangling.

Tom takes up the story. 'So, I was singing with The Senators in this club in Cwmtillery called the

Top Hat Club,' he said. 'It sounds very posh, but it wasn't! So, we were playing there and Gordon with his wife came and saw the show. When he saw it, or heard me singing, he said, "My God, you should be in London!" And I said, "I understand that, but who do I talk to when I get there?" And he said that he would help me. He wasn't thinking about management at that time. But he said he was writing songs for Leeds Music, a music publishing company, and he would do whatever he could. He called me another night and said that he was thinking about management. He said he'd never managed anybody before because he was singing with a group called The Viscounts up to that point, and he had had some success with writing songs.'

Actually Tom already knew of Gordon Mills, which gave him some confidence, as did Gordon's track record. Apart from his time as a singer, he had also had some success as a songwriter, which meant that he knew all the different aspects of the trade. 'He wrote "I'll Never Get Over You" for Johnny Kidd and The Pirates, and he wrote a song for Cliff Richard,' said Tom. 'Cliff had a hit with one of Gordon's songs so he was doing well as a songwriter. So he said he would like to manage me if I was up for it. And I said, yes, definitely. Because I knew who Gordon Mills was, I'd seen him on television, so I knew that he knew what he was talking about. He wasn't one of those guys that said he could do something and then he couldn't. I mean, I knew this man could.' He was right. Gordon did, once famously telling him, 'You just sing. I'll do the rest.'

A few preparations had to be made, starting with his name. There was already a Tommy Scott in London, so a new moniker was needed, and fast. Tom's real name, Woodward, was felt to be not quite right. But finally Gordon Mills had a stroke of genius: a new film had just been released starring Albert Finney, which was receiving a huge amount of publicity. Why not take advantage of that and give him the name of the film, *Tom Jones?* And so a legend was born. On Gordon's part this was a very canny move and a sure sign that Tom had finally got the right person to help him on his way. The various stop-starts up to this point certainly hadn't hurt him, too, for they gave him a certain resilience necessary for any performer who has a career spanning decades and an ability to bounce back; they also helped him keep his feet on the ground. Even now, Tom has never made the error of believing his own publicity: while he has talent by the sack-load, to get to where he is now takes a great deal of luck, too. He has always acknowledged this and never denied how fortunate he has been.

Even so, it was not all plain sailing – it took a while before a record deal came through, a time that was to prove miserable for the young Tom. He was scruffy and perceived by many records companies to be too 'raw'. He and the band were living in London's Notting Hill on the £1 a day paid to them by Gordon, which was less than the average wage in 1964, while back in Wales Linda was still working. He really considered giving up. 'There was only one time when he wavered and that wasn't because he was thinking about himself,' said Freda Woodward. 'He had come home for Christmas. "Mum," he said, "I think I'll just have to throw it in and take up work again." He felt really bad about his wife having to work to keep the home fires burning. I said, "Don't worry, it will come out all right. I know you can do it." "Do you really think that, Mum?" "Yes, just be a little patient."'

Times were so tough that on one occasion Tom actually stole a steak from a passing waiter at a trendy club where they had all gone to be seen. Indeed, for one very brief moment, he even contemplated ending it all. He was on a platform on the London Underground when it occurred to him how easy it would be to jump. 'For a split second I thought, aww, f★★k it! If I just step to the right it'd be over,' he said. 'I felt so down because I didn't know what to do. That very rarely happens to me. I didn't want to go back to Wales without proving myself. I wasn't making any money. F★★k it! But then things flash through your mind. What about your wife? What about your son? What about your mother and father, how would they feel? But for that split second, that's as low as I ever got, just before "It's Not Unusual".' But he didn't jump.

Ironically, it was just a few weeks after that when Tom signed with Decca record label. They had not forgotten their initial interest in the young man with the astounding voice. But what was needed now was a hit. For all the power and magnificence of his voice, Tom still had to channel it into the right material and this was not immediately forthcoming. Indeed, his first single, 'Chills and Fever', released in 1964, sunk without trace. But Decca knew what it had on its hands and the company determined their new singer was to make the grade, and so plans began for a second, follow-up single. The choice, 'It's Not Unusual' (1965), was not an obvious one. For a start, it had originally been intended for the singer Sandie Shaw and, in its early state, was very much more watered down than Tom's version would become. Written by Gordon Mills himself, it had been recorded as a demo with Tom singing. He immediately latched on to it, exclaiming, 'I've gotta have that song!' Although Gordon was unsure as to the wisdom of this, Tom persisted and eventually got his way.

There were still more boundaries to overcome. The song had been written for Sandie Shaw and the next task was to ensure that she would be happy if it went to someone else. In the event she was extremely gracious. 'God bless Sandie Shaw,' said Tom, decades later, 'because she said, "Whoever is singing this demo should put it out. I can't sing like that."' And so it was that the song was altered to suit Tom's macho style and released. Even so it was not plain sailing. Had it not been for pirate radio, Tom might never have made his big breakthrough and the world would have been deprived of one of the twentieth century's greatest entertainers. The BBC considered the single so raunchy they didn't want to play it but pirate station Radio Caroline was made of sterner stuff and gave it airtime. Decca was quite right: on 1 March 1965, 'It's Not Unusual' went to No. 1 in the charts. It caused an absolute sensation.

Freda Woodward had previously heard the song

and knew there was a chance it wouldn't be released. 'If they do, you've got a winner,' she told Tom. And they did. 'We heard it one morning on the radio,' she said. 'Then a few days later a little lad down the road ran up and said, "Mrs Woodward, do you know that Tommy's record is No. 21 in the charts?"'

'No. 27,' Tom Senior corrected her.

'That's right,' said Freda. 'He said it was No. 27.'

'It then did a big jump into the Top Ten,' said Tom Senior. 'When it came out in the papers that Tommy was No. 1, the neighbours kept running up all day, saying, "He's done it! He's done it!" It was marvellous, and that night we had a party and tasted champagne for the first time.'

The speed of his success caught even Tom by surprise. 'I was on a package tour with a lot of bands and I wasn't aware that "It's Not Unusual" was going so fast up the chart,' he said. 'We used to do two shows a night. So between shows I went to the pub and I was having a pork pie and a pint, and these girls were outside screaming. I thought they must be here for one of the rock bands on this package, but they'd all gone back to the theatre; the kids must think they're in the pub. So I walk out the pub, straight into this crowd, with a pork pie in my hand. And they go "Oooooo" and they're on me! And they tore everything. I had this raincoat, the first decent raincoat I ever bought, and it went like in f**king shreds. I had to run to get back in the theatre.'

It was proof, right from the start, that here was a force to be reckoned with, and the reaction from

39

the girls made it clear that Decca now had a serious sex symbol on their hands. Tom had not had a formal training, but he possessed a certain raw quality that made him stand out from the crowd. Not only this, but his quite exceptional voice brought the house down wherever he went. And so almost overnight he was catapulted from a complete unknown into mega stardom. Given how suddenly it all happened, it was quite a change to cope with, but he managed. And he was certainly different from anyone else around in Britain at the time. 'He has a very earthy appeal,' said one music industry analyst. 'When he first burst on the scene, the charts were full of skinny young pretty-boys. With his strapping build, hairy chest and tight curly hair, Tom was the complete opposite. But it was soon obvious that he appealed to ladies, who liked a bit of meat with their veg.' It was an interesting way of summing up his appeal, but undoubtedly true.

At that early stage of Tom's career many patterns were emerging that were to become part of his life throughout his career. For a start, it was not widely known that there was a Mrs Tom Jones in the background. Keen that he should appeal to as wide an audience as possible, Tom's managers encouraged him to deny that he was married, something he duly did. Of course, it then came out almost immediately that not only was there a wife but also a son in the background, one who was now eight years old. And so, on 1 March 1965, the day 'It's Not Unusual' went to the top of the charts, Tom confessed that Linda was waiting for him back home. Indeed, he seemed nothing but relieved that his secret was finally out.

'I was told by my managers, publicists and everyone around me to say I was single,' he revealed. 'I was not happy about it because it's not true. I am married. When I came to London I was told to say I was single. I knew that sooner or later the secret would come out. It's never been a secret back home in Wales that I was married. But when I came to London it was felt best if my wife and son were dispensed with. I should never have agreed to say I was single in the first place. When I sing, I sing from the soul. And I sing from my heart – you can't fool teenagers.'

The song duly made No. 1, Tom's fans coped with the fact that he was married and his roller-coaster ride to fame began in earnest. 'Bookings for performances came in so fast from all round the country that I doubt if I could have told you the day of the week,' he recalled, some years later. 'It is a rule in showbusiness strategy to cash in on a success and we were doing that as hard as we could. Life became a bewildering succession of stages, stage-door crowds to be escaped from in disguise, reporters, photographers with flashing cameras, snatched meals and crazy drives across the country.' He, of course, loved every minute of it.

Such sudden success meant logistical problems had to be tackled swiftly, too. Tom's old friend, Chris Ellis, had driven the band around in the early days on a part-time basis. 'We were seldom on time because the van kept breaking down,' he once said. After that first hit he was asked to become Tom's full-time road manager and he accepted the job. 'Tom did not have a car of his own for some time,' he recalled, in 1969. 'Then he bought a new Jag. I was with him the first time he took it out. At a roundabout, Tom hit another car. His driving has improved since then, but he usually prefers to let me do the driving. Now it's a Rolls, and he has to sit at the back with darkened windows up, otherwise there would be autograph hunters waiting every time we stopped at the traffic light.'

Delighted with the success of the song, Decca realised it had a major star in the making and released three more of Tom's singles that year. 'Once Upon a Time', 'Little Lonely One' and 'With These Hands' didn't do quite so well as 'It's Not Unusual', but they were perfectly creditable and had the effect of building up his career. His first album, *Along Came Jones*, was released in the summer of 1965, and along with the songs by Gordon Mills and Lou Reed, featured numbers written by Jerry Lieber and Phil Specter ('Spanish Harlem'), Wilson Pickett ('If You Need Me'), Chuck Berry ('Memphis Tennessee'), Johnny Mercer ('Autumn Leaves') and Brook Benton ('Endlessly'.)

Along Came Jones was released in the States under the title *It's Not Unusual*. On the cover, in blue jeans and red shirt Tom stands, looking moody and almost unrecognisable from the man of later years and indeed, this was one of the last sightings of his original nose. It's still possible to see the early, raw Tom in his features, but he was learning – and changing – fast. The boy from the valleys was metamorphosing into a metropolitan sophisticate who would soon be taking the world by storm. By this time it was also becoming clear to him that he was going to have to leave Wales and move to London full time. His feelings about this were very mixed: on the one hand, all these great opportunities were opening up to him and yet he was leaving the land of his fathers. In recent years he sounded quite wistful about the fact that Charlotte Church was able to stay put: 'She likes Cardiff and it's great if she can do it,' he said. 'In the sixties you had to move to London because there was no M4 and the quickest way to London was by train.' And so move he did, now taking his family with him.

As his profile increased, Tom stepped up his touring, first in the UK before going on abroad. He has fond memories of those years. 'The first thing I remember was going up to Scotland to play the Glasgow Apollo and my organ player was driving,' he said. 'We stopped at the side of the street and asked this guy directions and I couldn't understand a word he said. After we found the Apollo, it was a great experience. I remember doing a soft ballad and during a little gap in the song, a girl loudly sighed, "Och, Tom!" I could hear it cutting through the air and I started to laugh. It broke me up and destroyed the mood, but it was so funny and so Scottish. I've toured all over the world, but Scottish people in general never mess us about. They tell you exactly what they think. And for me, not being English had a lot to do with the Scots accepting me.'

More major hits followed, as Gordon cleverly

had Tom record the music for two films. The first of these successes, in June 1965, was 'What's New Pussycat?'. The second, in December of the same year, was for the latest James Bond movie, *Thunderball*. Of course, Bond and Tom Jones were made for one another: had the spy been real rather than fictional, he would almost certainly have bumped into Tom at a Las Vegas casino, checking out the women and deciding which ones to go for. (And Bond wouldn't necessarily have won.) It was certainly very prestigious, too. At the time the Bond movies caused as big a sensation as Jones did himself, and anyone chosen to sing the theme tune was considered much honoured. Tom himself was delighted.

'You know, there's a lot of movies now with a lot of special effects and stuff,' he said, years later, recalling how he was asked to sing the Bond theme. 'But they are still making James Bond movies. But then it was new. Sean Connery was James Bond and all those special effects were all new then to film-making. So if we could get a Bond song to go with the film that was fantastic. Shirley Bassey did *Goldfinger* (1964), which was very successful for her, Matt Monroe did *From Russia with Love* (1963), which was very successful, and then I did *Thunderball*. So it was great, you know, to get a Bond. I was glad that they asked me. John Barry and Don Black wrote it. I was thrilled when they asked me to do it, and it was a huge success.'

It also was the source of an almost certainly apocryphal story. Tom ends the song on such a throbbing, drawn-out cry of 'Thunderbaaaaaaaaaaall!' that stories circulated that he had passed out after the recording. That is almost certainly not true, but it is an indication of the power and strength of his voice.

Tom's next record, 'A-Tom-ic Jones' came out the following January and shortly afterwards, another person instrumental in forming his image and guiding his career came on to the scene: Chris Hutchins. He was to become second in importance only after Gordon Mills in Tom's career at that point. Hutchins identified exactly what was needed to project him to the public in a way that would build on his charisma and sex appeal, something that, despite all the Rock'n'Roll and tight leather trousers of the early years, had always been played down. Indeed, Tom was very much presented as a family man. An astute PR man, Hutchins decided that from now on, Tom's status as an attractive man should be brought to the fore, whereas his marriage and child should not be emphasised. There would be no more cosy domestic interviews. Indeed, to begin cultivating an air of mystery, there should be few interviews at all.

Hutchins, who was at that time working on the *New Musical Express,* was spot-on in his perception. He arranged a meeting with Gordon Mills and put forward the new strategy, after which he was taken on for the initially small sum of £25 a week. While the change in image was to work magnificently, at the same time, it had a huge effect on Tom's marriage, for again Linda was edged out of the picture and this time she stayed in the shadows. Indeed, many people believe the reason she has become so reclusive is down to those early days when it was put to her that public knowledge of Tom's marriage would hold him back. According to some sources, it is a message that not only has she never forgotten, but she continues to act on to this day.

Certainly, Hutchins's strategy could not have been better for Tom's career. The cosy home shoots became a rarity, while he adopted a far more overtly sexual image than ever before. There were several different stages to come before he finally found the niche that he was to occupy for the next four decades, but the stage had been set for the rise and rise of Sir Sex Bomb, an image he maintains to this day.

CHAPTER 3

TOM, THE VOICE

A legend was beginning to take shape. Throughout the world, Tom's fame was spreading, as was his raunchy reputation. In Australia, some newspapers branded him obscene because he removed his shirt in the middle of the act. Other countries also treated him with caution. But he took it with a pinch of salt. 'It was very funny, really,' he said. 'When I went on to *The Ed Sullivan Show* in New York [in 1965], the producers said, "Now listen, son, keep it cool. Move sideways only, otherwise we'll black you out, wrap it up." In Brisbane a copper came into my dressing room, poked me in the chest and warned me, "Now listen, you, this is a clean town and it's gonna stay clean. Any trouble from you and we'll shove you inside. OK?" I felt like butting him in the nuts, but me hair had just been combed for the act.'

Four decades on, he remembered the time as one of relative innocence. 'It's just me,' he said, of the hip writhing that has carried on right into his sixties. 'Looking back, it wasn't that racy anyway – not compared with what goes on today. It was just nice to move about a bit, you know. I remember the first time I went to Australia in 1966. The police filmed the show so they could decide whether they should cancel the tour or not. I was doing a move called "The Jerk" and they said, "What are you doing with all that thrusting?" And after I appeared on *Blue Peter* the BBC received letters from housewives asking, "Who is this man gyrating in front of my daughters? It's disgusting!" They asked me to tone it down the next time I went on!'

Of course, he never did anything of the sort. What might be termed the 'raunch factor' was an enormous part of his appeal and again, there was no one else in Britain with an act quite like his. The sixties heart-throbs tended to be somewhere between coolness and hippiedom, but none of them quite had the raw, full-on sex appeal exuded by Tom Jones. And it helped that this was not an act – Tom has always famously had an eye for the ladies. All he needed to do was to make that clear on stage and he was away.

As the scale of his success became apparent, he

himself began to try to analyse just what he'd got – and everyone else didn't have. 'I've got to be able to grab 'em and not let go,' he said. 'This is me singing, you see. I'm trying to get across that I'm alive – all of it, the emotion, the sex and the power, the heartbeat and the bloodstream is all theirs for the taking. You see, man, all the other singers are really only imitations of Elvis Presley. I don't go for them at all.' It was, however, put to him that he was not above a little pelvis rolling himself. 'Agreed, agreed – but the words don't mean as much unless the body gets into the act,' said Tom. 'Al Jolson got on his knees, Danny Kaye makes with the hips, the best coloured singers move, man, move! I admit I shove it a bit but I don't spell it out like Presley. It's the emotion that triggers off the body.'

There was one person, though, who was determined that Tom's growing success would not go to his head. 'My mother keeps everybody's feet on the ground,' he said. 'If I get a bit airy, like, she says to me, "Listen, Tommy boy, you may be a big shot up in London but down in Pontypridd you wipe your boots when you come in, you're good to your wife and you take turns bringing in the coal." Mind you, she's real chuffed with my success. She loves it when the neighbours drop in with autograph books.' The whole family was loving it, having a bona fide star. Seemingly he could do no wrong. At that stage, his audience was very much the teenybopper crowd: young girls screaming, shouting and then losing interest as soon as their new-found idol wasn't there, as Tom found out to his cost after he spent three months touring the United States. In many ways the visit was a success as it began to establish him overseas, but it had a disastrous effect on record sales back home.

The unthinkable happened: Tom's next three singles flopped, and with it came a real worry that his career might be over even before it had begun. 'Fear crept in,' he said, a few years later. 'Looking back now, I am very glad it did. I realised it was not safe to depend on teenage audiences whose interest apparently can only be sustained with hit records. I had to look elsewhere.' What happened next could not have been better thought out, or more beneficial in the long run for his career. Indeed, it was the basis for a career that would last decades rather than a couple of years. Tom turned to his agent, Colin Berlin, for advice, and he suggested that he should start to appeal to an older and more sophisticated audience. He should move his sights upwards a decade or two and market himself to adults, change his image from heartthrob to sophisticate. Tom did as he was advised, and it worked.

'Colin Berlin, my agent, found the answer when he booked me on a tour of northern nightclubs,' said Tom. 'Until then my act had been a frantic thirty-five minutes with everyone screaming. Now I had to appear on a floor surrounded by people at tables. I had to introduce myself and my group, and I had to do it before sophisticated audiences. I remember telling Gordon Mills, my manager, I did not think I was quite up to it.' But he was, and quite spectacularly so. His first gig was in La Dolce Vita nightclub in Newcastle, doubling with another club in Stockton, and with an audience quite different from the one he was used to. It was a sensation. 'The tour broke all previous attendance records at the clubs,' said Tom. 'This gave me a wonderful feeling of confidence. It meant I did not need to be in the charts to draw customers.'

That said, he had no intention of giving up on making records and work began on the next single. But this time, the record was to have that older and more sophisticated audience in mind. It would be a ballad and Tom had just the song in mind: 'The Green, Green Grass of Home'. The rest, as they say, is history. To this day it remains the song with which he is most associated, the common understanding being that in it he sings longingly of the Welsh valleys. He may be, but the song means nothing of the sort. First recorded by Jerry Lee Lewis in 1966, he sang longingly of the green, green grass of the American Deep South. No matter, the song served its purpose and was a phenomenal hit.

And it came about, like so much else, by chance. 'I've always been a big Jerry Lee Lewis fan,' said Tom in an interview with the BBC in 1999. 'I was in New York in 1965, and I had gone into this record shop called Colony Record Shop to ask did they have Jerry Lee Lewis's latest album, whatever it was. And it was the first country album that he had made. It was called *Country Songs for City Folk*. So I bought it. And I went back to the hotel and I played the album on a little record player that I used to carry around with me, and I heard this "Green, Green Grass of Home". I thought, my God, that is a great song, that.'

Initially, though, Tom had not necessarily thought of releasing it as a single. Instead, he decided to feature it on TV and make a clever scenario to surround it. 'I came back to England, and I was doing some TV shows, in black and white in those days, and I did "The Green, Green Grass of Home" on TV,' he said. 'And we did it like in a jail. But you don't know it is a jail until the camera pulls back because it's about a man in jail. So the camera pulled back, you see the bars, and I'm in this jail, singing "The Green, Green Grass of Home".'

That first airing proved invaluable in that Tom actually got audience feedback before the single was released. It was a rare opportunity – singles were usually released completely cold. Given that he was in the process of changing his style it was a much-needed confidence boost before he made the final decision. 'The following day I go to get the car filled up with petrol and the fellow on the pump said, "Oh, what was that song you did on the telly last night, when you were in jail?" he recalled. "That's a fantastic song!" So I thought, oh, you know, it has had an effect. Then different people were coming up to me the following day, saying how much they liked this song that I sang in jail. So they didn't know at the time it was anything, but everyone was getting affected by it.'

Tom approached Peter Sullivan, his recording manager, who was at first uncertain about him releasing the song as a single. For a start, it was a country song, a totally different genre from anything he'd done before, and even if he was aiming at an older audience than previously, country music was not necessarily the way to do it. But Tom knew what he wanted, and so the decision was taken to give the song an arrangement that would make it more mainstream. The result was a spectacular success. If anything, he was more popular than he had ever been, yet with an older, wider and more durable fan base. It was one of the best decisions of his career.

'I said to Peter Sullivan, my recording manager, "Look, I'd like to record this," he recalled. 'And he said, "A country song?" I said, yeah, because I hadn't done a country song up to that point. And he said, "All right, if you want to give it a whirl, we will. So Les Reid did the arrangement, and Les made it more of a pop song than a country song, because when Jerry Lee Lewis did it, it was strict country. When I did it, it was a bigger band with strings on it, and more of a lush arrangement to it. To get it sort of mainstream, as we used to say. So we did, and it was a great arrangement, and it worked. It came out and it went to No. 1. So that was my second No. 1. "It's Not Unusual" was the first in '65, and "The Green, Green Grass of Home" came out in '66, which was my second No. 1.'

It was a fantastic achievement and, more importantly, it was one where Tom had followed his instincts. He was beginning to sense what worked for him and how he could change songs and meld them to fit his image. His manager and the team surrounding him bore a great deal of responsibility for what was happening to him, of course, but he himself was showing considerable flair. 'I just liked the song,' he said. 'I thought it was a great song.

And there was a twist to it, you know, when you are singing about the green, green grass of home, but then it's about the man who is in jail. And he says, "I realise I was only dreaming." He was dreaming about home. So I had this picture and me coming from South Wales, of course, I thought of my home, which was Wales.

'But I thought it was only affecting me that way. I had the picture of Wales and being green, you know, the green, green grass of home to me was South Wales. But then everyone else thought the same thing. When the record came out, first of all they thought it was a Welsh song, that someone had written this song for me about Wales. But then I realised it is about anybody's home because it never mentions the name of a city or a town, or a country or anything. It just says, the green, green grass of home. Which could be anybody's home, whoever is listening to it thinks about where they come from, and in my case, it was South Wales.'

Money started coming in, too. In 1966 Tom earned about £100,000, a phenomenal sum in those days, and he celebrated by buying his first Rolls-Royce. Hit after hit followed: 'Detroit City', 'Funny, Familiar, Forgotten Feelings', 'I'll Never Fall In Love Again', 'I'm Coming Home' (all 1967) and, of course, 'Delilah' (1968), another song with which he will always be indelibly associated.

'It's a passionate love song, "Delilah," he said in the 1999 BBC interview. 'You know, so much so, that it's about a woman that cheats on a man and he kills her for it, you know with a knife. "I felt the knife in my hand, and she laughed no

53

more..." It's just that, because of the melody, it's not a ballad. I think that if it would have been a ballad, then people would have realised what it was about more. But it's because of the melody, and because of the arrangement, you take it as a sort of tongue-in-cheek thing. It is not as violent as the lyrics suggest because of the way I sing it and the arrangement.

'So people sing it as a sort of drinking song, because that's the way the melody goes. It's almost like "Those Were the Days", that Mary Hopkin had. And that's what "Delilah" has become. I know they sing it at a lot of Welsh matches, which is great. But it is more, because of the chorus it's more of a drinking song, a sort of a sing-along that people can sing. But the actual story of it, of course, is about him killing his girlfriend. Which is not the happiest of subjects, but it doesn't seem to matter with that song.' It was another example of Tom putting his personal touch to a song.

Strangely enough, it was the only time the subject matter of the song caused a problem related to the sexual content and not the violence. 'When I went to do Delilah on there [*The Ed Sullivan Show* in New York] a couple of years later, they said they had a problem with the lyric,' Tom related. 'So I said, "You can't take out 'I felt the knife in my hand and she laughed no more' – it's part of the song!" And they said, no, it was not *that* part they were objecting to. I said, "Well, what else is there? If it is not the knife, what is it?" They said, well, "At break of day when the man drove away, I was waiting." I said, "Well, what is wrong with that?" They said, well, if it was at break of day, when the

54

man drove away, that means he was with her all night. I said, "Well, of course he was – that is why she gets killed. That is why 'I felt the knife in my hand' because she was with this man all night."

'And they said, you can't sing that on national television. You can't suggest that this woman has been with this man all night. I said, "Well, why the hell do you think that she gets killed for it?" So I had to say, "At break of day I was still cross the way, I was waiting." I said, "OK, fine. You know if that is what you want. I mean, it was so bloody petty. But they wouldn't... The thing that struck me was they didn't care about her being killed; they cared about her sleeping with a fella. I mean, it's stupid.'

Such small irritants apart, he could hardly believe his success and admitted he still worried it could all come to an end. 'Only trouble is, I get these nightmares, see,' he said in the late sixties. 'In my dream, I'm back at the beginning. I see this agent and he says, "We can only pay you sixteen quid for a show." Now I'm screaming, "But listen, man – I'm pulling in a couple of grand a week! I don't work for sixteen quid!" Boy, am I glad when I wake up and I can see the Rolls-Royce through the window!' It was typical Tom – honesty, combined with a self-deprecatory joke that made it quite clear how wealthy he was becoming.

Increasingly, the success of Tom Phase II became apparent, and he himself felt it, too. 'When I first came to London, my act was very wild, jeans and that, and I used to come leaping onto the stage and go bang, bang, straight off,' he said. 'I realise now you can't expect an audience to be

55

ready for the big stuff until you've warmed them up. For another thing, it was at the height of the Beatles and I was trying for a sexy image, and I was too old for the sexy image – well, I looked older than them.'

He continued to build up his new persona. Having survived the northern circuit, summer 1967 was time to take on the south, most notably The Talk of the Town, then London's best-known cabaret club. He may have had some success already but again, he was a bag of nerves. If he succeeded here, his future on the cabaret circuit seemed assured. In the event, all went well.

'[I was] scared,' he revealed later on. 'On my opening night, nearly everybody who mattered in the pop music world was there to see if my cabaret act lived up to my records. The act lasted fifty minutes, which I thought was too long, but the applause, which still rings in my ears, told me I had been able to hold their attention. Las Vegas, New York, Miami and the West Coast of America followed.' The tour was a resounding success, establishing him as nothing beforehand had done as an entertainer able to last the course.

That venue was also a host to one of Tom's more unusual shows. Once asked what was the oddest gig he'd ever played, he replied, 'It was The Talk of the Town, in London. Ben E King was a friend of mine, and he was coming to see me and I thought, great, because it was a great venue. When he came in, I told him, "You're gonna dig it." But then Gordon said, "I forgot to tell you, the show's been bought out tonight by a male convention." I replied, "But there's gotta be women

56

in there, right?" He said, "No, no women. It's a stag thing. There's nothing you can do about it, they bought it." So I thought, shit, Ben E King, great soul singer, coming to see me and I gotta go up and sing to all men, which I hadn't done since I worked in this club in Wales with people that I knew. It was strange to come out on stage and see the place full of men, but as it turned out, it was a great show. They dug the shit out of it.'

By 1967 Tom, Linda and Mark had moved to Shepperton, just outside London. Their home, a three-bedroom semi-detached, was modest compared to what was to come, but palatial given what they had been used to. It provided a refuge for Tom, somewhere he could retreat to from the increasing bustle of the outside world, where Linda was always waiting for him with a decent meal. 'I always seem to be in the kitchen,' Linda confided in what was becoming a rare insight into the marital home. 'When Tom comes home he is always eating!'

But not cooking! 'I can cook, for instance, but I won't,' he said. 'It's not a man's job. I like women to do a woman's job. I'd hate to come home and not find Linda here.' There was little chance of that. In later years, Linda became very reclusive, but there were signs even back then that while Tom went out and partied, she was content to stay at home. She did not go out without him when he was out on tour, nor did she accompany him to showbusiness parties on his return. 'When Tom is here, it's nice just to have him to ourselves,' she explained.

This was, in fact, one of the last-ever interviews

given by Linda, in 1989. As her husband's career advanced, she had become accustomed to staying in the background, although she had, until then, still been happy to speak out in public from time to time. However, she found that her words were often misrepresented or misquoted, and as a result of that, she began to withdraw more and more. 'She was so excited about owning a house and having our son with us and money to spend,' Tom said. 'She did interviews and would have her picture taken with me but often she would be misquoted and I'd say, "What the hell have you said?" So she stopped doing interviews and became reclusive.'

Nor was it just the media from whom she began to withdraw. At the beginning of Tom's career she had friends who were married to members of his entourage and she would spend her time with them, and even go out and enjoy herself with them when Tom was away. But she began to stay away from them, too. 'I think they started getting on her nerves because their husbands were away with me and they'd moan the whole time,' said Tom. 'She said she didn't want to be reminded that I was away.'

But the family was clearly happy, for all that Tom now spent so much time away and the couple appreciated a standard of living that had once seemed impossible to come by. 'After we were married, we lived with my mother in a terrace house with no bathroom,' Linda told one interviewer. 'We used to have to get up at five in the morning, so that Tommy could be at work by six at the paper mill. And we would dream of a house like this. Just think – I was twenty-one before I even set foot outside Wales, and now I'm living here and we have visited America and Spain, places like that.'

Even so, there was a downside to Tom's new-found fame. 'As soon as I came to England, I felt Welsh, you know,' he said. 'I miss Wales, I miss my mates. And these days I miss not being able to go into a pub with Linda and just sit quietly drinking a pint without being on show all the time.' And he was – at home as much as anywhere else. The Shepperton home housed a huge collection of stuffed cats sent in by fans after the success of 'What's New Pussycat?' while his admirers were also known to make off with pieces of furniture from the patio outside. 'Sometimes I would like to set this house down in a field on its own,' said Linda, in another foreshadowing of the more reclusive life she was to choose in later years. But the Joneses were still charmingly proud of their new abode with all its mod cons. Tom happily chatted about choosing the colour of the carpets – gold in the bedroom, blue on the stairs, brown in Mark's room, brown and white in the guest bedroom and green downstairs. 'I can't stand green, yet I am always buying it,' he said. 'I've got a green Rolls, too.'

At the time his words might have sounded like boasting but in retrospect there is innocence. These days it's very hard to imagine Sir Tom Jones talking about choosing the colour of his carpets, let alone glorying in the ownership of a three-bed-room semi. Yet back then, having risen so rapidly from a very poor background to what must have seemed like enormous wealth, what came across was the sheer pleasure to be had in it all. And at that time, Linda was as happy to give interviews as her husband. She was utterly thrilled with their home, confiding she preferred carpeting to bare floors, and fussing about the central heating. 'The warm air heating blows dust everywhere, too,' she said. 'Tom likes the temperature high – up at seventy-five.'

In 1968 another part of the Jones legend fell into place: women started to hurl their knickers at him. Like so much else, it came about by chance. 'I was booked into the Copacabana in New York,' said Tom. 'An American agent had seen me at The Talk of the Town in London in '67 and asked me if I wanted to play the Copa, and I said, "Yeah, America, why not?" So we came in '68. It was a club where there's no stage – you're singing on the dance floor on the same level as the audience.

'So, I'm doing my thing, and I perspire when I sing, and these women are handing me these table napkins, and I'm wiping myself and giving them back. Then all of a sudden one woman stands up, lifts her dress and takes her panties off. You learn when playing in rough places to try to make the most of it. Don't get offended, don't get thrown. So I said, "Careful not to catch a cold." All of a sudden it was written up in the papers, and there's underwear all over the place. But the original thing was a sexy thing.'

By the end of the 1960s, Tom was leading a private existence with Linda and Mark on the one hand, and a public, career-driven one on the other. Now he was regularly playing Las Vegas, where he was pictured in the Flamingo Hotel meeting a man with whom he had something in common, both in looks and in their music: Elvis Presley. And as a sign of his growing status, although he had been avowedly an Elvis fan before now, it was Elvis who had come to Tom's concert rather than the other way around.

In actual fact, the two men had met a couple of years previously in Los Angeles and immediately hit it off. 'We were both at Paramount Studios – he was doing a film and I was recording a song for a movie,' said Tom. 'He heard I was there and apparently asked if he could come and say hello. I couldn't believe it. Just six months before I was skint and listening to Elvis records at home. When he came over he said, "How the hell do you sing like that?" I told him he was partly to blame.'

Another person Tom met back then was John Lennon, but the two did not bond quite so well. (Elvis, incidentally, hated Lennon.) The occasion was the rehearsal of the television show *Thank Your Lucky Stars*. 'I was with my manager, waiting for The Beatles to rehearse because I wanted to see them,' said Tom. 'When John Lennon came on to the stage, he saw me sitting there and sang, "It's not a unicorn, it's an elephant," to the tune of "It's Not Unusual". He said, "How are you doing, you Welsh poof?" I replied, "Come up here and I'll show you, you Scouse bastard!" I was cross, I thought he was teasing me, making fun of my record. I thought he didn't like me. He told me to f**k off. I later realised it was his Liverpudlian sense of humour. I thought The Beatles wrote great songs, but their music didn't impress me like Elvis Presley's did. Lennon said himself that he wrote commercial music.'

Tom took to Vegas, and vice versa, immediately. Always something of a man's man, he relished the macho atmosphere of the place and right from the start he understood there were shady elements to the place, as well as some very tough characters. But that just made him fit in all the more. He also got on extremely well with his fellow performers, who were happy to offer advice to the newcomer. Tom was well aware what a fortunate man he was.

'The first time I went to Vegas was in 1968 and we have played there every year since, so I think I have played Vegas longer than everybody now, including Frank Sinatra,' he recalled. 'It has changed a lot since the sixties. Back then you were aware that there were hoodlums running around, but it's not like that any more – it's cleaner than clean. I know a couple of shady characters from New York that go to a Vegas restaurant. I said to one, "Why don't you come to the show?" and he said, "I'm afraid I can't. They won't let me in because of my prison record."

'Back then the guys running the casinos knew that I was from a working-class background and that I was a self-made man. That goes a long way. We had similar backgrounds but took different roads in life. They are very much aware of that, and if you are a stand-up guy, you'll be all right. It was there that I got praise from the established giants in the business telling me they loved the way I sang and that was a great thing for me. Elvis and Sinatra both told me that. Sinatra said I should be doing big band stuff and turn to jazz.

I said OK. Then Elvis said he thought I was making a big mistake. He said, "We don't do that." I'm glad he said "we". "We leave that kind of thing to Sinatra," he said. I told him I liked to do different kinds of music, but it was great to think I could get advice from two legends like that.'

CHAPTER 4

TOM JOINS THE GREATS

Just a few years previously, it would have been almost unthinkable, but now Tom really was right up there with some of the greatest entertainers of the twentieth century. It was no longer strange to hear him described as being in the same league as Elvis and Frank Sinatra, and it was not just his voice that catapulted him into the arena of the greats. Of course, without it, Tom would never have got anywhere, but he had all the other necessary attributes of a truly great entertainer, too.

For a start, he was extremely charismatic. As with all true stars, he only had to walk on stage for the attention to be focused on him and then when he did start singing – well. The women in the audience would go frantic, and even the men enjoyed it, too. Women wanted to bed him, men wanted to be him. Tom had stepped into a whole new territory and made it all his own. As his fame and fortune continued to grow, he and his advisers worked hard to cultivate his image, one that is to all intents and purposes with us today. The trousers got tighter, his shirts were buttoned lower, and jewellery, especially medallions (excellent for highlighting all that chest hair) began to make an appearance. Tom was adept at striking a pose, more often than not with a hat tilted at a rakish angle and a cigar clamped firmly in his mouth. He was beginning to acquire the patina of an international star. Although he has never lost his Welsh accent, his image was now increasingly transatlantic. Indeed, he was forming a strong attachment to the States, one that would endure. Although he was never to take out American citizenship, it is where he has lived for the greatest part of his adult life.

Above all, he was enjoying his fame. There would seem to be two types of entertainers: those who take to success like a duck to water and those who are ultimately destroyed by it. Frank Sinatra fell into the former category and Tom's great friend Elvis into the latter which, given the similarities between the two performers, could have been an ominous sign for Tom. But he never fell into any of the traps that eventually destroyed Elvis on 16 August 1977. He never took himself too seriously, he never believed in Tom Jones, the Myth; he always remembered where he'd come from, he enjoyed his success without becoming overwhelmed and, most importantly, he never took to drugs.

It is the pragmatic side of Tom's character that is most obvious here. He had been handed opportunities rarely accorded the rest of us and he was determined not to mess up. In recent years, he has been prone to talk about his voice as a God-given gift, but even back then, there was a sense in which he realised quite how much had been handed to him.

He was forming a strong attachment to fellow performers, too, especially Elvis. Tom was often to reminisce about his friendship with the King, and indeed, it was a bond that would last right up until Elvis's death. On another occasion, he told BBC Radio, 'The first time I met Elvis was in Los Angeles in 1965 – the first year, my first successful year. I'd met all the British groups first, because I did British television before I went to America, so meeting The Beatles and The Rolling Stones and all these famous bands at the time was great in itself.

'Then I go to America and I meet Elvis Presley. And the first meeting was, I went to Paramount studios in Hollywood to talk about a song for a movie, and they said, Elvis is here today filming and he would like to meet you. So I thought, my God, I didn't know that he knew that I existed, because I had three singles out and one album at the time. And that was "It's Not Unusual", "What's New Pussycat?" and a ballad called "With These Hands".'

For Tom it was still new, but it was a world to which he quickly adapted himself. Some find fame a burden, but right from the start he enjoyed it, taking to the lifestyle and enjoying what his money could buy. He also revelled in his meeting with Elvis, the entertainer with whom he had so much in common. Both were from poor backgrounds, both had overwhelming voices and both were susceptible to the charms of the fairer sex and enjoyed enormously all the accompanying boys' toys their positions would bring.

'When I got on the set where Elvis was filming, he got out of his helicopter,' Tom recalled. 'It was like a mock helicopter for the film, and he walks towards me and he's singing "With These Hands", which was my record. I couldn't believe it. It was like a dream, that Elvis Presley was singing my song, you know, to me! We had a picture taken, and I told him how much an influence he was on my singing style.'

The two men really had hit it off. They started chatting immediately, with Elvis quizzing Tom about his background, obviously wondering (with some reason) if Tom's country of origin produced a lot of people like him. 'He said, "What's it like in Wales, then? You come from Wales?" he remembered. 'I said, yeah. And he said, "Do all people sing like that in Wales?" I said, "Well, not exactly," but I said, "Welsh people have strong voices, that is where I get my strength from. My volume is where I come from. But," I said, "I was influenced more by American music than I was Welsh traditional music."

'So I said, "It's a combination. I have a Welsh voice but because of American music influencing me so much, I am sounding like I do." Because they thought I was black, you know. When they first started playing my records in America, they thought I was black. And so did Elvis Presley. He said, "When I heard "What's New, Pussycat," I thought it was a black fella singing it." Which was strange for him to say because they thought he was black when he started.'

The friendship was a deep and inspiring one, with the two men understanding the type of life each was now to lead. 'We became friends from that day on, and that was in '65,' said Tom. 'We were friends until just before he died. We worked Vegas a lot together, at the same time. He came to see me at The Flamingo in '68, because he said he wanted to make a comeback, live, because he hadn't sung live for years. He wanted to sing in Las Vegas, so he felt that I was the closest thing to him; I had a similar approach. My stage presence, he felt, was very similar to his. So he said to me, "You were very successful in Vegas, I want to watch you, I want to see what you do." And then it gave him more confidence to make a comeback.'

It was quite something, after just a couple of years in the business, to be the inspiration for one of the most famous singers of all time, but that was indeed what happened. Encouraged by his friend's success, Elvis decided to make a return to the stage. 'He saw me in '68 in The Flamingo, then he opened the International Hotel – no, he was the second one in, Barbra Streisand opened it – and Elvis was the second one in to the International in 1969, which later became the Hilton,' said Tom.

'He said that I gave him confidence to make a comeback, because the group thing was so big, he felt his style might be old-fashioned. The single performer, you know, was gone because The Beatles were so successful. And he said that because I was so successful, it gave him more confidence to make a comeback, which I was very pleased about, that I had contributed something to Elvis Presley, because he had contributed so much to me, and the world in general, of course, in the '50s. Being influenced by Elvis, I was glad that I could give something back to him.'

It was then very much a man's world. Both Tom and Elvis had women hurling themselves at them, but they were never part of the inner sanctum. They were there to entertain the men, to provide glamour and, of course, after-hours comfort, but they were never treated in the same way as the men. This was a world in which the men gambled, drank hard, worked hard and played hard. It was a world of boys' toys, of casinos and alpha male jousting. Even so, there was one huge difference between Tom and Elvis: while Tom had a rock-solid marriage in the background Elvis did not. Tom might have enjoyed the wine, the women, the fripperies, but his relationship with Linda was grounded in a totally different world, a real world, with values that, to this day, the two continue to hold. Despite his marriage to the beautiful Priscilla, which ended after a few years in divorce, Elvis didn't have anything like that. He had hangers-on who indulged him, whereas Tom always had a sense of what Linda would think about what he was doing, even if he managed to quell it pretty successfully for extended stretches. Though she may have chosen to be in the background, Linda always brought Tom back to earth.

That is not to say that he did not thoroughly enjoy the other sides of life that Las Vegas had to offer, too. To all intents and purposes, he was leading a bachelor lifestyle, revelling in his new-found status. Having come from such a poor area with so few opportunities, he was not about to complain about the pressures of fame. Anyway, he didn't have a problem with them. He liked having fans, he enjoyed being recognised, he loved the applause and, not unnaturally, he adored the success.

His stage routine was now as polished as they come and he absolutely loved the fact that he was a sex symbol. It all added up to a great deal of contentment, but never arrogance. Indeed, it is that which has probably contributed to the length of his career: the fact that Tom always remembered where he'd come from and despite his unquestionable talent, the fact that he'd had a lot of luck.

He was quite unabashed about how he liked to spend his time, talking about visiting the nightclubs to watch all that was on offer. 'One night [in 1968] we decided to look at a few burlesque strippers at the Silver Slipper,' he revealed gleefully. 'And then this incredible girl comes on to the stage. She's dressed like a cat. She climbs up on to a stool and looks down at us. This woman had no business stripping anyway because she didn't have a very good figure. Chris Hutchins – my road manager – screamed, and all the fellows who were looking at her broke up in laughter. I said, "Shut up, for Heaven's sake!" But he wouldn't. It was a great laugh and I'll bet that girl went down better that night than she's ever done before.'

But sometimes even he seemed taken aback at the loucheness on display. 'A theatrical agent came backstage another night and asked, "What d'you want to do? There's a good topless show down the road with lots of beautiful girls." I said, "It's not one of those cheap strip things, is it?" I didn't want to see any more middle-aged women undressing. He told me they were all lovely young girls. That was different. "It's a classy show," he said. "I know it is because my wife's in it." So we went along and stayed there. Yes, a good show, too. But I felt quite embarrassed looking at the girls. I didn't know which one of the topless ones was his wife. But it didn't bother him at all. I didn't meet the agent's wife.'

'I did,' interjected Chris Hutchins, who was present at the time, with a grin.

It could not have escaped Linda's notice that by this time her husband was spending a great deal of time away from home, working in a business peopled with beautiful women. And it seems she took a pretty pragmatic approach right from the start. When he was once asked how they had stayed together despite his many extra-curricular activities, Tom replied, 'We trust one another. She told me early on, "I don't want to read anything in the papers, to see anything, but one thing I don't want is you running away with another bird." If you love one another and trust one another, and know you're going to be together, then your marriage is solid,' he said, adding, 'it's not a conventional marriage, though.' Despite this, it is a marriage that has endured.

Of course the big question is one that has never been answered because Linda has not given an interview for about forty years. Did she mind? She wouldn't have been human, had she not. After all, when she and Tom got married, there was no hint of what was to come. No one had a clue what shape her husband's life was to take. Former local tearaway Tommy Woodward married his pregnant childhood sweetheart, but went on to carve out a life for himself, a life which was not the one for which Linda had signed up.

She had seemed to enjoy his initial success as much as he did, but as time went on, it became apparent that Tom's career was going to create two very strong challenges to their marriage. These were the amount of time they spent apart and the temptations presented by other women and rarely turned down by him. The realisation that life in the wake of his success was going to be more difficult than it had first appeared must have been hard.

It was in the 1960s that Linda seemed to begin to disappear. The lively young girl from Wales, Tom's childhood sweetheart, was starting to be replaced by a much more guarded woman, who knew but could not face the fact that other women flocked around her husband as bees to honey, while he did nothing to brush them aside. So, when did this realisation set in? It must have been at around that time, because Tom, for all his talk about not wanting to hurt Linda, has never been particularly discreet. He would clearly have been appalled at any suggestion that he was being cruel to her in any way. Indeed, to this day, he cannot accept that her reclusive nature may have anything to do with him, but it is hard to escape the conclusion that, at that stage in his life, he was going to have his cake and eat it, too.

And he did, over and over, and openly at that. At that time newspapers were kinder than now to straying celebrities, but even so, the rumour mill was turning over full steam about what Tom got up to in his spare time. No one close to him on tour was under any illusions. He didn't get his reputation for being a stud entirely by chance.

What is unquestionably the case, though, is that Tom has always been at the absolute centre of Linda's life and so to lose that grounding would mean not just the loss of a husband who she clearly loved – and who also loved her – but an entire way of life. Without Tom, what could she do? She, too, had left working-class Wales behind. Whether she liked it or not, Wales was no longer home and never could be again. She and Tom had stepped outside the realms of the life most of us lead and into an extraordinary mode of existence involving great wealth, fame and travel. While Linda might not have wished for any of these things, she was stuck with them by virtue of the man she married. To have left Tom would be to cast adrift, and where would she have gone from there? Besides, she didn't want to leave him and so she accepted her lot, and began on a modus operandi that continues to this day.

As for Tom – well, Tom was Tom. He also had a pretty unique perspective on what led men to mess around in the world in which he lived. 'There are more temptations for men in show-business because it's like a reversal of roles,' he said. 'Women are always pursued, whether they're famous or not. That doesn't happen to men, even good-looking fellas, because girls don't know anything about that. But when you're on television or in the movies, they feel they know something about you. That's why so many men stray. They have a hit record and wow! I started singing at school and clubs and women went crazy.'

Even now, the women still go crazy, but back then it could hardly have failed to be intoxicating stuff. Tom adapted to what happened to him extremely quickly and well, but his rise in the world of celebrity had been so fast that he could be forgiven for getting too carried away with it all. Apart from the women, however, he didn't. Somehow, while loving every minute of what was happening to him, he managed to keep hold of reality. He never forgot where he came from, never forgot that he was lucky and never forgot that other people had also been responsible for his success. Many people, when they become famous, suddenly decide that they've done it all on their own, ignoring the publicists, managers, musicians and songwriters who have helped them on their way: Tom has never done that.

Still the friendship with Elvis endured. The two men revelled in the lifestyles they led and, in each other, had found someone with whom they could truly relax. Both were happy to take advantage of all that was on offer: after all, they were young, rich, handsome and in the biggest adult play-ground in the world. How could they not have fun? 'He'd be singing at the Hilton and I would be at Caesar's Palace,' recalled Tom of the late sixties. 'The only problem was that when he finished his shows he would come and see mine, and then he would want to party all night. The sun would come up and I would say, "Elvis, I've got two shows to do tonight. Go to bed!"'

And Tom certainly brought out the better side of Elvis's character. When he was playing Vegas, Elvis would, on occasion, take to the stage himself and tell the enthralled audience that Tom was the greatest singer in the world. On another occasion, the two men were in Hawaii, Tom on tour and Elvis on vacation. Elvis, wishing to play some music with Tom, realised he didn't have any guitars with him, walked into the nearest music shop and announced: 'Tom Jones is coming to my house today and I need two guitars.' Indeed, the two men often sang together and it is one of Tom's enduring regrets that those impromptu performances were never recorded for posterity, on the instructions of Elvis's manager. 'If I could have recorded with Elvis that would have been great,' he said. 'But [Colonel Tom] Parker wouldn't let him sing with me. Elvis never did a duet with anyone.' It would have been quite a pairing, but it was not to be. However, much later in his career, Tom was to record an album of duets that brought him to the attention of a new young audience, which fell happily under his spell as previous generations had done. But that was decades hence.

Another element of Tom's career that has served him very well is that right from the start, he surrounded himself with the best people in the business, everyone from his manager to his backing band. He was very aware of that too, always giving credit where it was due and understanding that all these people contributed to his own success. The compliment was returned in full. In 1969 he teamed up with a musician who was well known in his own right: Big Jim Sullivan, who played the guitar. Big Jim was to stay with Tom for five years and he certainly appreciated quite what a talent the singer possessed.

'I do think that Tom would have been one of the greatest operatic singers that ever lived if he had classical training,' he said. 'I have never heard such a powerful and tuneful voice in my life as a musician. When we rehearsed you could hear his voice over the top of the full orchestra. His pitch was total on every note and his feel for time and phrasing was impeccable. I know musicians from all styles had great respect for Tom. I have heard him sing the blues with a voice like Howlin' Wolf and BB King put together. The man is a total natural and very few people have this kind of talent. I only left Tom because my own way in life was not compatible with the life on the road.'

Others included Lloyd Greenfield, who looked after Tom's interests in the States, Les Reed, who acted as a composer, conductor and arranger and, eventually, The Blossoms. The Blossoms, who originally comprised Darlene Love, Jeannie King and Fanita James, joined Tom in 1971 to become his backing singers, an association that was to last for twenty-one years. They were extremely experienced musical professionals and as The Crystals they had had a hit with 'He's a Rebel' (1962), also providing backing vocals for Sam Cooke, Duane Eddy, Paul Anka, Buck Owens, Bobby Darin and the King, Elvis himself. Over the years, the line-up changed on various occasions, with Darlene Love, in particular, finding some solo success. And yet another was Johnnie Spence, who in 1969 became Tom's musical director, before sadly dying in 1977. Tom was one of his pallbearers.

There are many more people who contributed to his success than those listed above, but the point remains: Tom has always worked with the best in the business and he was sensible enough to listen to advice when it was offered. He has constantly adapted to suit the mood of the times, too. It is a pattern that has been repeated in recent years. Now in his sixties, he has never been afraid to perform with younger stars and has outshone them all.

Indeed, it is hard not to note the difference between Tom and his one-time duet partner Robbie Williams. Both outstanding stars of their age, Tom was prepared to work hard, get on with it, never complain, never explain, never buckle under the pressure, enjoy his stardom and always give credit where it is due. Robbie has not done likewise. It is also noticeable that when the two performed together, Robbie had never been better. He was forced to pull out all the stops to keep up with a man over three decades older and, talented as he is, he only just managed to pull it off.

Meanwhile, Tom's success just got bigger and better with every day that passed. His popularity continued to soar, while his professionalism ensured he never got too carried away with it all. Again, like Elvis, he not only had his musical and management entourage, but groups of women, too. It was practically *de rigueur* during the sixties for major male singing stars to have adoring females accompanying them, a personal harem of sorts for an evening on the town, and so women were constantly on the scene as an adornment to his playboy image.

As Tom grew increasingly comfortable in his luxurious new world, he became something of a connoisseur. Unlike Elvis, and his fried peanut butter and banana sandwiches, Tom's tastes were developing fast. It wasn't just the champagne, which continued to be his favoured tipple, but his standards of cuisine rose as well. So did his dress sense, and here he differed from Elvis, too. Circa 1968 Tom developed a look which, with various modifications, he still sports to this day – tight trousers, hairy chest, medallion or cross. It is an individual appearance, one that he has made entirely his own.

He has often been mocked for it, too, with gentle teasing about the tightness of the trousers (less so these days), and quite the breadth of the expanse of hairy chest, but he has never made himself look totally ridiculous. Elvis, alas, did. By the end of his life, his costumes were so over the top they had become a cliché, and he was not averse to appearing similarly dressed when he was not on stage.

The Senators continued to work with Tom, but by the late 1960s, as he concentrated increasingly on television work and Las Vegas, they simply weren't needed any more, and so they disbanded. There was also a bout of unpleasantness, rare in Tom's career, when former managers Godfrey and Glastonbury took him to court, saying they were owed money. By now, of course, the sort of fees Tom commanded and the fortune he was building up was considerable. Even before he moved to the United States as a tax exile in 1974, he was becoming seriously wealthy.

Given the pressures of time, fame, girls and the potential for misbehaviour, it could all have imploded – again, look at what happened to Elvis – but somehow Tom managed to keep his feet on the ground. He remained extremely close to his family and now that he had been given so much, he was determined to share it. As well as providing financially for them, he spent time with his parents and sister, which meant he never forgot his background. He continues to be extremely generous. His generosity and concern that everyone in his immediate family and environs is looked after is one of his best character traits.

Not that he didn't mind boasting but in the nicest possible way. Tom was inordinately proud of his houses, his cars and his general standard of living, so much so that it sometimes had to be played down. That oft-professed love for champagne, for example, is not something with which everyone empathised. At times there were jealous mutterings in some quarters about how far he'd come from his old rough-boy image, and it was inevitable that some men were jealous of him, too.

Tom could, and usually did have his pick of women. But such was his good-hearted nature, his ability to put himself down and his enormous popularity among those who knew him personally and others that admired him from afar, that the jealousy never became overtly nasty. He stayed in touch with his old friends, too, achieving that neat, but almost unfathomable trick of stepping into a new life without ever quite leaving the original one. Tom was still Tommy Woodward, a miner's son from Wales.

Above all, he remained a man's man. This is what kept the men on his side, as well as women. While women might have adored him, essentially he was still a man who liked to hang out with the lads. In the old days it might have been with the local crew, these days it was with Elvis Presley. This worked in his favour in Wales, in Las Vegas, on tour – it is part of who Tom is, and who he always will be. This was no manufactured image: his personality shone through and through, and only increased affection for him all over the world. In Britain he was a symbol of pride, one of our boys made good, and in the States and the rest of the world, he was simply the consummate entertainer, one who never failed to pull out all the stops. And life was to get even better...

CHAPTER 5

THIS IS ... TOM JONES

He was well on the way to becoming a legend. Before 1969, Tom's earnings were estimated at nearly £1 million a year, a truly colossal sum for the time, which meant his surroundings also changed to accommodate his new status. The family had outgrown their house in Shepperton and moved to Weybridge, Surrey, where they lived in a mansion that was then worth £65,000. Tom had not sold his first place: rather, with great generosity he gave it to his parents, Tom and Freda. He was helping to give all his family a new kind of life: his parents were also getting an allowance, he bought Linda's mother a house in Tonteg, Wales, and his sister Sheila and her husband Ken had been given a cottage in the grounds of the Weybridge mansion.

Tom and Freda were clearly delighted at his generosity. 'A lot of people think it's Tom's duty as our son to look after us,' said Tom Senior. 'But we don't. We think it's absolutely marvellous of him, particularly when you consider the way most boys drift away from their parents. Ken looks after the garden in Weybridge and I'm always on call to do any odd jobs and help out in other ways.

'It's certainly all a change. I was down the mines for forty years. When Tom became a success one of the first things he wanted was for us to get out. But I wasn't due to retire for another eight years, and at first I wouldn't come out. Freda and I wanted to make sure his success was going to last. Even so, it's a big relief now I'm out. Right up to the end I was still getting about fourteen tons of coal out a day, but if I'd stayed on, I would have slowed down. I've always worked this way, getting paid so much for every square yard instead of labourer's money.'

Indeed, life had changed beyond all recognition for Tom's parents, as well as for Tom himself. His parents were leading the kind of lives they could never have aspired to without his success and the two could scarcely believe the way they lived now. 'For forty years, I got up every morning at 5.15am,' Tom Senior told an interviewer. 'We had to be down the shaft in the cage before seven – it was a quarter of a mile down. I was very lucky and never had an accident, but many of my friends died.

'You really appreciate everything when you've been underground for all those years. You see things differently from other people, especially gardens. We always took our lunch down in tins, as otherwise the mice nibbled away at it. It was dark and there were huge spiders called Jaspers, but you always had your lamp. You worked hard down there.' But life had now changed. 'At the start we thought it was all a dream,' he went on. 'We couldn't believe it. But we feel secure now, we don't want for anything.'

There was, however, another side to this story. Tom has a generous nature with everyone and has lavished the money he'd earned on others quite as much as himself, but that was not the only reason he wanted his parents to move. His fame was having an effect on them, too. 'You know what it's like in a small place,' he said. 'They all know you so they think you're a load of no good.' (Tom has a very love-hate relationship with his birthplace.)

'Every time I was on telly or I'd a record coming out someone'd say to my dad in the pub, "Ooh, your Tom this" or "Oooh, your Tom that." My dad kept getting into scraps, going home with black eyes and that. I knew sooner or later some young lad would get at him and really do for him, and then I'd have to go down there and stick one on him, and it would have gone on from there. So I brought them down here. Nobody makes a fuss in Shepperton.' So, it wasn't just Tom who had to deal with jealousy and animosity – it was his father, too.

Not that his dad was complaining. And Tom Senior was gracious about the fact that, as the father of a famous son, often he was now called 'Mr Jones' rather than 'Mr Woodward'. 'We accept it,' he said. The couple were also delighted with their new life in the London suburbs. 'At first when we came I couldn't get used to the beer and I missed the men's clubs, but now we go down the local every day,' he said. 'People come up to us and talk about Tom's latest shows. Oh, we've made some good friends here. And we've been to the Palladium four times. We don't miss Ponty at all. Once we came down, we decided to make a complete break, so we've only been back twice.'

In 1967 Tom had to have his tonsils out, an operation which resulted in another development in his public persona. While it is his voice, above all else, that has set him aside from the pack, his image as a *bon viveur* has contributed hugely to his popularity. It was that year when Tom decided what were to be his indulgences and what were not. 'Before going home after the operation, I asked the specialist about smoking and drinking,' he said. '"If you want to sing, spirits and cigarettes are out," he said, "but you can drink beer or wine, and smoke a pipe or cigars." I settled for cigars and champagne. It must sound very opulent, but the champagne helps to give me a little lift before going on the stage.' It is hardly the advice a specialist would give now but, as the years were to prove, it worked for Tom.

By now he was so famous that almost everything that happened to him made the news – and so it was that he found himself the subject of one of Prince Philip's famous gaffes. After a Royal Variety Performance he asked Tom, 'What do you gargle with, pebbles?' a remark that was widely commented upon. But what really caused a fuss were his later comments made at a lunch of the Small Businesses Association, to the effect that he didn't think much of Tom's singing, or his gigantic earnings. Tom's singing was 'hideous,' he said, before going on to compare his salary with those of small businessmen.

Uproar ensued. Tom was an extremely popular singer and to impugn his singing did not go down at all well. It was said that there would be a letter from the Palace to explain the remarks. Then it turned out that Tom hadn't received any such letter. 'Tom has not contacted the police about the letter,' said a spokesman at his Mayfair office. 'He would not do this as he is not upset in any way about the remarks supposed to have been made about him by Prince Philip. I gather it is a friendly letter. Tom is taking it that way.'

His long-standing press agent, Chris Hutchins, who added, 'We have been told that the Prince was critical of Tom's singing and earnings. Tom took it as a joke. But he does pay enormous taxes on his earnings.' In a further twist, it emerged that his offices had been broken into, with thieves taking cash, stamps and fan mail. Was the Prince's letter among those taken? It wasn't clear.

In fact, Tom was less than amused about Prince Philip's remarks. He was prepared to say so, too. 'I wish I had known how he felt before coming to see the show,' he remarked. 'Someone would have paid good money to charity for his ticket. I wasn't giving an audition for the Duke; I was giving my services to a charity.

'I don't mind what he thinks about my singing – he's entitled to his opinion – but he is, in fact, running down the whole British entertainment industry, of which I am proud to be a member. Personally I have always spoken well of the Duke. When I go to America, I am often asked about the Royal Family.' With that he calmed down somewhat. 'If Prince Philip is still worried about not having enough places to stay, he can come and live with me whenever he wants,' he continued, now restored to his usual good humour. 'I am proud of the country I come from.'

The remarks had clearly hurt his feelings, though, for his manager, Gordon Mills, also spoke out. 'He is the biggest solo entertainer Britain has ever produced,' he said. 'But he started out in a small way by any businessman's standard. He has got where he is today by hard work and talent.'

As Tom's star continued to rise, plans were announced for his own television programme, *This Is Tom Jones*. It was to be an international effort, made in Britain, at ATV's studios in Boreham Wood, and broadcast in both the UK and in the States. This was a massive step forward in his career and one that he greeted with the same apprehension he had shown during the transition from teen idol to cabaret star. But it was that very awareness that he might fail that gave him an edge.

'My new TV spectaculars are a complete departure from anything I have attempted before,' he said, when the shows were announced in early 1969. 'As well as singing, I have to introduce, interview and perform with big, international stars – most of them very polished and experienced people. I am naturally worried, but Gordon Mills has trained me for this role and he's a very exacting taskmaster. I am aware of the dangers of sudden success, but having come up the hard way, I think I know where I am going. My success was due largely to the brilliant management of Gordon Mills.'

The compliment was returned in spades. Gordon Mills, now one of the most successful managers of the day, was not only looking after Tom's career, but also that of Engelbert Humperdinck. It was a job he took seriously. 'I've got a responsibility towards Tom and Engel,' he said. 'When they are doing the job, it's my duty to be there, too, wherever they are. You see, they're not just a couple of artists, they're my friends. The very first time I saw Tom, I was bowled over by his talent. And I'm still his greatest fan.'

Like Tom, Gordon came from a working-class Welsh background and became a soldier and then a bus conductor. It was while he was doing the latter job that he began to play the harmonica in clubs. 'In all that time, I used to have pipe dreams about success,' he said. 'I wasn't attracted by the

85

glamour of showbusiness, just the money. I used to see things I wanted, like big cars, and making it in showbiz seemed the only way I could ever afford them.' He ended up in London with a band called the Harmonica Gang, before moving on to an outfit named The Viscounts, while sharing a room with one Gerry Dorsey, who, through Gordon's efforts, later turned into Engelbert.

And then, of course, there was Tom. Gordon actually saw him on a trip back to Wales to visit his parents, when he went to a working man's club to see Mandy Rice-Davies perform. She was ill and so in her place Tommy Scott and the Senators came on – and Gordon met Tom. 'He had a great voice and he moved beautifully,' said Gordon. 'I'd always thought that there was nobody to beat Elvis Presley but this boy even then was better.'

Tom tackled the TV show in the same way as he had gone about everything else and was handsomely rewarded for his hard work and determination to the tune of £850,000 a year (remember, this was 1969). As in the past, it was his willingness to experiment and to be guided that made his next venture a success. He has never let any kind of arrogance get in the way of anything; he has listened to others' advice and been prepared to change direction when it was necessary, something that over the long term was to work massively to his advantage. 'He is so soft,' explained the show's producer, Jon Schofield. 'So malleable, I mean. He accepts direction without argument. TV technique is vastly different from self-presentation on stage. Tom knows and accepts this. He is an absolute professional.'

He was also well aware of quite what an opportunity this offered. As the years went by, Tom had become increasingly ambitious and although he was popular in the States, he was yet to become a superstar. The TV show would offer him that opportunity. 'You can get to more people on television than you can in anything else, except for the movies,' he said. 'That's the same thing; that's the similarity. For me it was television, to get across my versatility so that I could do all kinds of songs every week, for an hour on national television in America especially. Because I've had hit records in America, but you know it is hard to become a household name in America because it is so big.

'So TV was the way for me to go. I was thrilled when ABC Television asked me to host *This Is Tom Jones*. I was doing duets with people that I had always wanted to sing with, and it was almost like a trade-off because ABC was pushing for more middle-of-the-road singers, thinking that that's what the American public wanted to see on national television. Then I was pushing for Jerry Lee Lewis and Little Richard, and all these rock singers that I had liked in the '50s. So they let me have them on because I was having middle-of-the-road singers as well.

'But because of my versatility I was able to do duets with a wide variety of singers. You know, not only Rock'n'Roll singers, but swing singers, you know, and ballad singers and Rhythm and Blues singers like Wilson Pickett and Aretha Franklin. I did duets with all those people. So it showed my versatility more so than the records. Because when you make a record it is one particular song and that is the single, and then you make an album which shows some versatility, but when people actually see you do it on television, I think you can get your point across much easier.'

He could also see that a different kind of performance was required on the small screen. 'I used to go wild on the stage, I used to float on a cloud through the music,' he said. 'But you can't do that on television. And I don't want to do it any more in real life. Too many people believe in me, and I mustn't let them down.'

But somehow he was managing to keep his feet on the ground. Though Tom was clearly revelling in his fame and success, he hadn't let it go to his head nor had he started to believe his own publicity. This he firmly put down to staying close to his roots. 'One of the penalties of success is that life can become artificial unless you cling firmly to the things that are fundamental,' he said. 'Linda, my wife, and I have always kept in very close touch with our families. Once I became established in London I bought houses for both her mother and my parents, so that they could live near us.

'We all manage to get together over most weekends. With them I can be myself. Outside our own homes, there is only one place I can be comfortable – in Pontypridd. In Pontypridd I meet my lifelong friends. Sure, the children outside the school may line up on the mountainside opposite our old home in Laura Street when they spot my Rolls outside. However, to most of the people who know me there I am not so much Tom Jones the singer as Tom Woodward's son who does a bit of singing.'

Tom's parents were proud of the way he wasn't letting it go to his head. 'You know, he's never changed,' said Freda. 'He's the same Tom today as he was when he was a lad – always singing. He used to sing in his pram, nursery rhymes. Not a bit shy either, like many children who turn their faces to the wall if they are asked to sing.'

For his father, his son's success was bittersweet, bringing back memories of his brother. 'It's a great pity my brother George is dead,' he said. 'He would have loved to see Tom now. Sometimes when I hear Tom singing a ballad it brings George back to me. George loved ballads. He was chairman of the Entertainment Committee at the Working Men's Club. He would say, "Wait till your Tommy grows up, I'll have him in the club on that stage."

'I remember, Guy Mitchell was a great favourite of theirs. Our Tom and George would listen to his records and sing his songs together. Tom has taken after him in many ways. Like George, you can't stop Tom singing. I've seen Tom come back from a fortnight up in the north, dead tired, and go to bed for a couple of hours. Then he would get up for a bath and you'd hear him singing in his tub. When we lived in Pontypridd the neighbours would hear him through the bathroom window.'

Unsurprisingly, however, his parents remained concerned about their son, for all his worldliness and success. 'One worries, you know, but I suppose it's the same with every mother, thinking her son is something special,' said Freda. 'When he comes home, I often just sit and look at him. It's funny, but I find myself wondering if it's true or just a dream.'

It wasn't even remotely a dream, but all the same, it did have some downsides, as Tom was beginning to find out. Fame breeds envy and not everyone was thrilled by his success. He now had to learn how to deal with detractors, usually men, who were clearly jealous. 'Not so long ago, I called in at a transport café on the M1 for a meal,' he related in 1969. 'Before I'd been there a few minutes, a lorry driver came up and sneered, "Look, isn't this Tom Jones?" His mate, a big, burly chap, answered back in a loud voice, "All right, what d'you want me to do about it. Kiss him?" It's that kind of experience that spoils life for me. I like a mug of tea with the boys, but it's one of those things I can't do any more. It's the same with pubs. I can't stop anywhere for a drink any more. In fact, it's a luxury nowadays for me to go into a pub, unless it's my local in Weybridge.'

Alas, it seemed that even Tom's beloved Wales wasn't a safe haven any more. 'It used to be worse there,' he said sadly. 'It'd be great if I could go back to Wales and be myself, pick up where I left off, go for a pint and have a game of cards with my mates. But things have changed. We have all grown up. At first I'd go into a pub and ask, "Is so-and-so in?" If I didn't buy a round of drinks for everyone they'd say, "What a mean bastard he is with all that money!" If I did, they'd mutter, "What a flash bastard!" I can't win, whatever I do. Besides, my old mates have all split up, got married, gone drinking in different places. So I don't go back any more.'

But when he did, problems could arise almost everywhere he looked. On one occasion when

Tom was appearing in Cardiff, some of the men he'd known as boys turned up at the stage door. It was agreed that after the concert they'd all go out for a drink, a plan which soon became fraught with complications. 'The idea was to go out to find a night-club and have a drink,' said Tom. 'But a lot of them were drunk by the end of the show, so I was afraid of taking them anywhere. I thought they might take the place apart.

'Wherever I go, there'll always be someone who's rude. I'm often tempted to plant my fist in a troublemaker's face. But if I hit out, then I suppose my name will be in all the papers and I'll get a bad reputation. So all I can say is: "I can't fight – leave me alone." Unless my back was against the wall, that is. Then it'd be different. I'd use anything I could find to hit my opponent. It's a funny thing I have about fighting tactics. Of course, I don't like to fight because it's terrible when two people have to come to blows. But when it really happens, I believe the motto should be "All or nothing".'

However, that was not the full story. Tom acknowledged there was an upside to his position, too. 'The boys on the building site near our new home, they give me the thumbs up as I drive past,' he said. 'You see, I was a builder's mate myself, once. So I open the other eye and give it back to them. It's funny, you know, now I'm listening to Tony Blackburn's programme on my way to the studio whereas I used to listen to it going to bed.'

Apart from the odd gripe, he was also very aware of how lucky he was. Everyone commented on his professionalism and what a joy he was to work with. Unlike many other stars, there were no tantrums or airs and graces. He wasn't that impressed by people who made mountains out of molehills, either. 'Some of my mates in this business, they're always throwing their weight about and saying, they want this, they don't want that,' he said. 'It's just because they think people are stupid enough to let them get away with it. I say to them, "Hey, what's all this crap?" and they calm down. They say, "Oh, it's easy for you, it's your nature to take it all." It irritates me, that. How do they know it's easy for me? Look at Frankie Vaughan – he's so calm I sometimes wonder how he can manage to sing at all.'

This exceedingly refreshing attitude was to be found in other parts of his life, too. He was unimpressed by people who talked about the agony of fame. Rather, he took a very realistic and appreciative view. 'Being a star is much easier than not being a star,' he said in 1969. 'Oh sure, it all depends on you, the whole show and that. Big deal! The thing is, the audience have come specially to see you. They know you, or feel they do. They're ready for you, waiting to react. You haven't got to work at it.

'The hard bit in this business is being halfway down a bill and they've all come to see somebody else and they don't want anybody getting in the way. You've got to work really hard then, it's a sweat to make them like you. I reckon there's no real stress in showbusiness. Working on a building site, that's stress. Getting up at six to do something you hate having to do, scratching your pick out of the ice if it's frozen solid – that's stress for you.

And getting £20 a week. An office boy in London gets £20 a week.'

Despite the undoubted advantages of his position, Tom did work hard. He was on tour for a good six months of the year, working by night and sleeping by day, and was now putting in very long days for his television series, but compared to what he had seen his father go through down the mines, he knew he was fortunate. 'People in the business say to me, "What you do is hard graft,"' he said. 'Hard graft? They don't know what that is, some of them! Everybody says, "This series, it must be killing you." Off from home about eight and I don't sometimes get back until after midnight. I just go to bed and get up again. But there's no stress. I'm doing what I want to do. I love singing. It's no problem doing what you want.'

Of course, he was being extremely well rewarded for his work, which helped. Given the contrast with his younger life, he was enjoying every minute of it, too. 'It's great,' he said. 'I like knowing there's a lot of money there to spend on anything I like. I've never had patience with people who are always scrimping here, saving there. When I used to take sandwiches to work it was always meat, never cheese, like some of them. And if my boy wants some sweets, I say let him have some sweets.'

His television career was going from strength to strength. But to this day his wife has never seen him in concert because she can't stand the way women react to him. When the new TV show started to air, initially she felt much the same way. But on this one, at least, Tom was able to persuade her to tune in. 'My wife has been very patient with me, but I've been patient, too,' he said in an interview with a journalist who visited him on set in 1969. 'At first she couldn't bear to watch me on television, sitting in the room with me, in case she had to watch me kissing and playing around with a girl.

'At the same time, she couldn't bear not seeing me, so she'd go up to the other set in her bedroom. I'd try to explain to her, it means nothing, I say, it's just part of the act. Well, you've seen yourself, what it was like today, with all those girls in black leather outfits, on the motorbikes, while I sing "Riders in the Sky". Of course, they're meant to look as sexy as possible, but what effect can that have on me, when I'm trying to remember which camera I face for the next bit of the take? "Riders in the Sky" was the first song I ever sang in the pubs. I put it in the show for luck.'

Indeed, Tom was making a great effort to convince Linda quite how important she was in his life – and she remains so, despite his various liaisons since. Back then he was being urged to stay nearer Elstree, where the series was made, at the weekends, but he refused, saying, 'My wife expects me to come home, and however late I am, she waits up for me. Not that I am late these days. Besides, I like what I see of Weybridge, now that I have de-Beatled it.' (A reference to the fact that two of the Beatles had just moved out.)

That their relationship is strong has never been in doubt. After all, they met as poor children from the same village and it was Linda who stood resolutely by him when he first started out. Tom has never forgotten that. 'I always remind myself how Linda never stopped believing in me, like my mother,' he said, in 1969. 'That's why I go home every night and always plead with her to come with me on my trips. After this series is finished I am doing a three-month world tour, starting in Australia, and I am hoping Linda will join me in the States. Though she hated it, when I played Las Vegas. She says she can't bear to see the way other women look at me in public. But I can't help that, can I? But thank goodness she's getting much more understanding about the sexy bits on the screen. And she is very pleased with our new home, because it's got more ground around it, so it's really private. When we are there together, she says she feels safe, and if I have a day off, we just sit around and play LPs, American mostly, and it's fine between us. Just as it used to be.'

That's not to say that there were not tensions, as well. Many rumours surrounded Tom's life on the road, something he had to explain back home. 'I'm a married man,' he said. 'Everybody knows I'm a married man. But they're always waiting for you to slip. If I take an American girl to dinner – she comes over here and she's in the show and she says, "What's the best place to go?" and if nobody else crops up I say, "Come on then, I'll take you." You go in there with her and you see people's eyes pop and next morning there's a picture in the papers. So I have to tell my wife everything I do – she doesn't like it if she doesn't know about it and she sees a picture of me with another girl.'

By this time, in fact, the pattern was being set

that would last throughout his marriage. Tom went out and had a life in the outside world, while Linda stayed home and carried on in her own domestic set-up. There have been many that have queried how the marriage has lasted through the racier stages of Tom's life, but the fact is he never has any intention of leaving Linda, and has always let her know that. Furthermore, her home is her domain. Tom took that decision very many years ago.

'I tell my wife that she's the boss in the home, not me,' he said towards the end of the sixties. 'That's right, isn't it? When I was a kid, if I came home from school, it never worried me if my dad wasn't there, but at the pub or the miners' club. But if my mother hadn't been there, why, it would have been the end of the world. And my wife is always there, she is someone to come home to, and that's why I think she should have the big say over Mark, our son. He's eleven now, but I always tell him, "Now listen to your mother" and I never interfere.

'What do I want for him? He's very bright. He might make a comedian. The really funny thing is that he sings quite well, his mother says, but I've never heard him because he stops the moment I come into the house.' In actual fact, when Mark was grown up, he was going to take over as his father's manager, after Gordon's death of cancer in July 1986. But his early awareness of his father's world, the world of music, certainly didn't hurt.

CHAPTER 6

TOM, THE TROUSERS

It's hard to pinpoint the exact moment that Tom became as famous for his off-stage activities as he did for his on stage performances, but it was probably around the mid-sixties, shortly after he came to fane. There is something about him that is irresistibly attractive to women, and it's not just because he is famous. He has frequently commented on the fact that, as a star, he is in the unusual position of being a man pursued by many women, as opposed to the other way round, but the truth is that it is not just celebrity that gives him his appeal.

In the early days, and even now, everything about Tom radiated sex. He couldn't look at a woman without undressing her with his eyes. Even in his interviews with female reporters he was constantly pointing out that there they were, a man and a woman, and it was impossible to think that there wasn't some kind of vibe. And while some women might have been dismissive, most of them loved it. What could have come across as arrogance in another man simply appeared as raw, unabashed sex appeal.

Unwittingly or deliberately, Tom could fulfil so many roles when it came to female fantasy, too. To some women, he was a bit of rough from the valleys in Wales. To others he was a charmer, a sophisticate who was at home anywhere in the world but particularly on the Las Vegas stage. He mixed in exalted circles yet stayed in touch with his roots; he presented himself as a real man, and then of course he was extremely handsome. Although he had not been born with the looks he came to possess, a combination of a skilful surgeon, exercise and iron self-will (he might be a gourmand but he has never allowed himself to put on excess weight) meant his natural charisma was now allied to a handsome demeanour. It was hardly surprising that women fell at his feet.

And Tom played up to it. He didn't exactly present himself as a shy and retiring type. Instead, he courted the attention, gloried in it and encouraged even the most demure members of his audience to join in the fun. The tie would be deliberately loosened at just the right point, the jacket would slide off after an appropriate build-up and the audience would go wild. Having gone into such full-on mode on stage, it was hardly surprising that he found it difficult to calm down afterwards. The build-up of adrenalin in his act was enormous and he was bound to find some kind of outlet for it.

But it wasn't all about women. As his star rose steadily higher, so he began to have the kind of experiences laid on for the very successful in their field. Ceremonies were staged especially for him to attend. He had gained international recognition and as such, there were invitations for him from all over the globe. One in particular touched him quite deeply. In 1969 he went to Germany to receive a Golden Disc. This meant he had sold 1 million records in Germany, bringing the world wide total up to 26 million. Stephan Braunlich, PR supreme at Teldec (Tom's German record label), had the brainwave to stage the reception in the salt mines of Berchtesgaden, southern Bavaria.

The thinking behind this seemed to be that Tom had been a miner, which was not entirely accurate (it was his father who had spent his life under-ground) but that didn't matter to anyone. Several truckloads of journalists were shipped in to watch the proceedings, which in the event went remark-ably well. First, there was a train journey from Munich to Freilassing, during which time he held court in one of the carriages. Afterwards he was escorted in a Mercedes to the mines, where a TV crew was in attendance. Escorted by a quartet of blondes, Tom got into one of the trains leading down into the mine and, as it arrived in a cavern, a band suddenly started playing 'Delilah'. His face was a picture. 'Going through this tunnel, I thought, what the hell am I doing here?' he ad-mitted later. 'And then to burst out into this great open space and the brass band playing "Delilah" – it was one of the most memorable experiences of my life!' He was presented with a miner's lamp and, ever diplomatic, he said it reminded him of the ones he had seen in Wales.

It was a world away from his childhood. He was now leading an international life, at home in all quarters of the globe, especially the States. No longer a British star made good, his name was now up with some of the greatest entertainers in the world. He was invited everywhere, recognised everywhere, idolised by women and respected by men – he was indubitably at the top of the show-business tree.

His television show proved extraordinarily popular, bringing him to an even wider audience than before, and he was also a rich man. And not only was the Tom Jones of the late sixties and early seventies now totally unrecognisable from Tommy Woodward, he was unrecognisable from the young Tom Jones. Long ago his nose had been reshaped; he was more stylishly dressed than ever and now there was an added sophistication to him. He had learned the importance of appearance in his profession; he worked hard not only to maintain his voice, but also to keep his powerful physique. Given that he liked champagne and good living, a will of iron had to be maintained to keep his figure trim. Tom, whose only idea of exercise in the early days would have been a good dust-up after a night in the pub, was learning to look after himself.

It wasn't just big, corporate experiences that he enjoyed, either. Every aspect of the entertainment industry appealed to him, from the highs of being on stage to the ensuing publicity circus. These days he could strike a pose with the best of them and lapped up press coverage. He also wanted to show his appreciation to his fans. They would frequently come to visit him while watching the show, and Tom would make time to see as many as he could. 'If it's at all possible, I have them in to the dressing room, one by one, or two or three at a time if the queue's long,' he said. 'For real fans I can't do enough – it's them that made me. What I can't stand are people who just happen to see you in a pub or somewhere and they say, "Give us your autograph, then," or they tell you where they think you're going wrong.'

The fans who queued up to see Tom during the TV show were the gentler variety, however, while the ones he encountered singing in concerts and at nightclubs were altogether more predatory. By now, throwing panties had become an established part of the proceedings and it wasn't uncommon, when he was singing in places like Las Vegas, for women to throw him the keys to their room, too. Tom was adamant it was all a show on the part of the women. 'That's as far as it goes,' he said. 'If I really went after a girl in the theatre, I'm sure she'd run a mile.'

It was a tactful comment, but as time wore on, he did less and less to deny what really went on behind the scenes. The reality was very different. It was estimated by a member of his inner circle that Tom bedded about 200 women a year while on tour, and if one didn't respond to his blandishments immediately, he would simply move straight on to the next. Of course, as his reputation for womanising grew, it became self-perpetuating. Women knew what to expect from him even before they met him, which did nothing whatsoever to harm his chances later in the evening. If you got backstage to see Tom Jones, then you weren't too surprised if the evening took a turn for the interesting. And if you didn't want that kind of outcome, you simply stayed away.

All of this would have been perfectly well and good, had it not been for the figure of Linda in the background and she cannot have been thrilled by the turn of events. Ironically, her existence gave

Tom the excuse he needed to behave as he liked with all the women he encountered and never make it serious. If a girl took a particular liking to him and wanted to take it further, he was often happy to do so, but he was adamant that ultimately he would return to his wife. It is difficult to say whether Linda should have adopted a stronger line from the beginning. The fact was that Tom was away so much there was no way she could have checked up on what he was doing. Even if she did, there's nothing to say that he would have stopped. He had discovered that he needed to do practically nothing to attract a new woman every evening, and had Linda put her foot down, it is entirely likely they would have split up. Neither of them wanted that, so she let him get on with it, turning a blind eye. In return, he at least made some attempt to be discreet.

While rumours persisted, they did nothing to dent Tom's popularity in Britain and the States. At one point, six of his nine albums were on the Billboard chart, and four had gone Gold. Hits kept flooding in, among them 'I (Who Have Nothing)', 'She's a Lady' and 'Tom Jones Live at Caesar's Palace'. His TV show, which was shown on America's ABC Channel was scoring high ratings and his concerts were doing better than ever. He did another four-week season in the Flamingo in Las Vegas for which he was paid $280,000 (£150,000) and the shows sold out. When he played the Copacabana in New York in 1968, queues formed outside at three o'clock in the afternoon. All this, and he wasn't yet thirty.

By the end of 1970 his position as one of the

most successful singers in the world was beyond doubt. By now he had sold 30 million records worldwide, while his TV show was going from strength to strength, attracting most of the major stars on both sides of the Atlantic, from Aretha Franklin to Bob Hope. Never bashful at the best of times, Tom's singing had become even more assured. Looking at him at the turn of the decade, it would have been impossible to believe that less than seven years earlier he had been a complete unknown.

The role of his manager Gordon Mills should not be forgotten, either. It was he who discovered Tom and he had been guiding his career ever afterwards. Tom was certainly aware of what a debt of gratitude he owed: his relationship with Gordon was now so close they were more like brothers. The two men had been made for each other, and it was a bond that would only be broken by Gordon's death.

Over the next few years, Tom became something of a permanent fixture in Las Vegas and, with Linda not present, living a bachelor lifestyle. In reality he had been doing so for some years, with stories of his many conquests increasingly rife in showbusiness circles. According to him, there was never any question that the two had an open marriage but at some stage Linda must have clearly realised, whether she ever admitted it to herself or not, that certain accommodations would have to be made if the marriage was to continue. She was now showing the reclusive tendencies that were to become more marked as the years went on, and at this time two Toms seemed to emerge: Tommy Woodward and Tom Jones. Linda herself once pointed out that she married the former, not the latter, and so while Tommy Woodward would always return home to his wife, Tom Jones led a raucous lifestyle, encompassing numerous lovers and hi-jinks galore.

Indeed, raucous is understating it. Women absolutely adored Tom and pursued him everywhere he went. He took full advantage of it, too. As has been stated, one member of his inner circle put his conquests at about 200 a year and some of the flings actually became serious. Throughout it all, however, there has never been any question that he would leave Linda, or vice versa. In fact, although his wife certainly wouldn't see it like that, being married was in some ways a safety valve for Tom. Again, while he was prepared to have sex with vast numbers of women, he certainly wasn't going to commit himself to a single one, even when the affair appeared to be more than just a fling. Ultimately, though, that is all any of them were.

In recent years, he was asked how many affairs he managed to have, to which he gave a very honest answer. 'I have no idea,' he said. 'I have never kept count.' Nor had he thought that it would ever put his marriage at risk. 'It's never discussed,' he said. 'She never asks where I am or what I'm doing. She never says, "You've got to call me." It doesn't come up in conversation. She doesn't question me or go into those things because if she did, she might find out something that she didn't like. We just go with the flow. She has never wanted to leave me and I have never wanted to leave her. We've never had to consider it. I don't think, I hate this woman and I've got to get away from her. She is happy with things and so am I. She wouldn't want it any other way. I have never been in love with anybody but my wife.'

It was comfort, of a sort. But, again, if Linda didn't want to lose Tom, there was nothing else she could do. What's more, she hadn't been brought up to deal with the kind of problem confronting her now. Tom and Linda come from a background in which the man's word is law and, however feisty she might have been, Linda simply couldn't impose her will over that of her husband. It just wasn't how she had been brought up. Of course, her upbringing didn't take into account the fact that her husband would not be working in the valleys of Wales, but instead she found herself in a situation in which any woman would have struggled to cope.

Tom, meanwhile, was in a different world. In those days there was quite a circus going on and no shortage of girls to hang around. Any pop star would have attracted a great deal of female attention, or to put it another way, groupies, but Tom was far more attractive than most. Sophisticate he may have been by that time, his raw, earthy quality never left him and women absolutely loved it. The panties throwing continued apace (and sometimes included bras and various other items of lingerie), all of which merely added to the charged atmosphere around him. And this was the permissive society in full swing. In the sixties and seventies, the Pill had made it easier for women to get it on as never before and people like Tom were the beneficiaries. London and elsewhere was swinging, and who could blame him for being tempted? Barriers were coming down and new modes of behaviour growing. Nowhere was this more evident than in the court of King Tom.

The changing nature of the times could have been made for him. Now women were happy to have sex outside the boundaries of marriage and so, too, was Tom. For him, it was the perfect time in more ways than one. Changing social attitudes made it possible for working-class boys to break out of straightened circumstances and reach the very top of their chosen careers and combined with changing attitudes to sexuality this turned some parts of society into a sexual free for all. Tom revelled in it; he loved it. The only rule was that there weren't any rules any more. Except one. He would have nothing to do with any married woman, out of respect for her husband and from the innate feeling that promiscuity was a man's, not a woman's game. For him, marriage was an inviolable state. It was a condition that worked very much to the advantage of men, who got to have a wife at home and girlfriends outside, but he would not seek destroy the domestic harmony of another man. And he didn't. Other men's wives were strictly out of bounds.

Of course, with so many women making themselves available, some attachments did form, although none lasted and nor was there any suggestion whatsoever that he wanted to leave his wife. Some of the names linked with Tom were famous in their own right: there was an American model called Joyce Ingalls and the singer Nancy

Wilson. But the first of his really big relationships was with Mary Wilson, one of The Supremes.

The affair, one of two big relationships in Tom's life, other than with Linda, began in 1967. In her biography *Dreamgirl: My Life as a Supreme*, Mary recalled how it was one of her booking agents, Norman Wise, who said that she and the singer should meet. Initially dismissing the idea, Mary then heard one of Tom's records and, like many before her, assumed he was black. Her interest began when she found he was not. She then saw a picture of him and, impressed by his good looks as well as unaware of the fact that he was married, she decided that she would like to meet him after all. After various delays, the big moment finally arrived when Tom came to knock on her dressing-room door. The attraction was immediate and intense. After more delays, one of which involved Tom being whisked off in a limo alongside Richard Burton and Elizabeth Taylor, the couple finally managed to spend some time together at the end of the evening. Champagne and kisses followed. 'By the time the evening ended, I knew I was in love,' Mary wrote.

So, in as much as he could be, was Tom. In later years he denied point blank that he had ever been in love with any woman other than Linda, but people who saw him at the time tell a different story. This was not just another fling: Tom was far more open about what was going on than he had been previously, and seemed suspiciously pleased when others began to realise that the two were a pair. And what a combination they made. Both were massively attractive, brilliant singers and

107

famous all over the globe. Ultimately, Tom chose to stay with his wife, but it must have seemed in many ways as if he'd met his perfect match. It is a well-known fact that when a man rises from a position of obscurity to great success he frequently trades in his first wife for someone he feels befitting his new status and that, however briefly, was what seemed to be happening here. Unlike Linda, Mary was part of his world. She understood it; it did not intimidate her. Like Tom, she was a world citizen, travelling constantly, rubbing shoulders with the glitterati. Although she never achieved anything like his fame, Tom must have felt as though he'd found a female version of himself in her.

It seemed that Mary, too, felt the same way immediately and fell for Tom on the spot. She, too, must have felt that she was with someone who understood the business she was in, the pressures and the pitfalls, and all that aside, the physical attraction between the two was immense. At the time, most women found Tom enormously attractive, but for a woman with whom he clearly had a real understanding, the effect was devastating. The two fell head over heels in love, the only problem being that the world soon got to know about it, too; as did Linda.

To begin with, though, the couple gave the impression of scarcely being able to think straight. Mary was also perceptive about exactly what it was that constituted Tom's appeal. 'This was really love at first sight, but much more,' she recalled in *Dreamgirl.* 'Tom loved women and his reputation as a sex symbol preceded him, but he was a man's

108

man. Despite his recent ascent in showbusiness, he retained the basic values of his working-class Welsh upbringing and always spoke his mind, no matter who was around to hear it.' It was this, according to Mary, which made Tom so very popular among his peers. He would tell it to them straight, something that appealed particularly to Elvis.

There followed the kind of relationship that can only exist among the very rich. Both Tom and Mary had their own careers to pursue, yet the two were besotted with one another, flying across the world to meet for trysts between gigs. It was glamorous, romantic, exciting and ultimately impossible to maintain. Mary had also become aware of Linda's existence, but by now she was in too deep. And so it went on: the relationship was an open secret in showbusiness circles, so much so that the most fashionable people at the heart of London in the Swinging Sixties would hold parties for them. Indeed, so open did the secret relationship become that references started to appear in gossip magazines. Mary, naturally, was cast in the role of home-wrecker, while Linda could hardly be unaware of what was going on. Matters came to a head, of sorts, in 1968 when Tom played a season in Bournemouth and Mary, to all intents and purposes, moved into the house where he was staying, something the newspapers soon got hold of. They lost no time in spreading the news.

'Back home in Shepperton, Linda was idly flicking through a copy of a music magazine when she came across a gossip-column paragraph disclosing the fact,' said Chris Hutchins, recalling the time.

Unusually for her, Linda decided to confront her husband. Perhaps she realised that, unlike the women before her, Mary Wilson actually constituted a threat. This was no one-night stand: it was an ongoing relationship, in which emotion, as well as physical passion, was being invested and Linda was going to have to fight for her man. She rang Tom in the rented home, where Mary picked up the phone in the bedroom and handed it to Tom. 'Hello,' he said.

'You, get that cow out of there now!' was the response.

And he did. Mary, like others before and after, was packed off the minute there was a suggestion that the marriage was under threat, although that was far from the end of the affair. For months afterwards matters continued in exactly the same way until finally, Tom told Mary there was no future in their relationship and broke it off. Somehow the two remained friends, with Tom going so far as to take Linda backstage to meet Mary after one of her shows. So why didn't he leave Linda? Clearly, there are plenty of reasons, not least of which is that he has always genuinely loved her and never wanted to leave the marital home. But it was also possible to see Tom's working-class Welsh background making itself felt here. Divorce was simply not an option in the world he came from. Besides, although Mary understood the world he lived in now, no matter how perceptive she was, she would never, unlike Linda, be intimately acquainted with his previous life. Theirs had been an intense passion while it lasted, but unlike his marriage to Linda, the relationship simply didn't have the depth that would have withstood breaking away completely from every standard with which he had been brought up. If Tom had left Linda at that point, in a funny sort of way, he would also have left Wales, something he has never wanted to do. Of course, there was also Mark to consider. Tom has always adored his son, and whatever his failings as a husband, there has never been any question that he was not a brilliant father to his first child. They were a tight-knit unit – Tom, Linda and Mark, and had been from the day he saw his newly born son in hospital. No matter how much he might have cared about Mary, he wasn't going to jeopardise that.

Mary is sometimes spoken of as the great love of Tom's life, but while he undoubtedly had strong feelings for her, that description is incorrect. Linda really is, and always has been Tom's great love, and examining the situation, it is not difficult to see why. Many commentators have not been kind about Linda's appearance in recent years, although in her youth she was a pretty, sparky and highly popular girl, but that is not the point. The girl next door from Wales was always going to win, despite the competition that included singers, beauty queens and models too numerous to mention, for the simple fact that she *was* the girl next door from Wales. Other than his parents and sister, Linda was the only person who knew who Tom really was. She understood his background because it was her background too; she knew where he had come from, the forces and influences that had shaped him and what it had taken to become what he was. Everyone else, his management team included, even Gordon Mills, only knew Tom from the time he decided to make it as a singer. Linda knew him from the days when he was a tearaway about town, a rough miner's son with no real future and nothing going for him but a strong voice. Back then, no one knew where that voice was going to take him. No one else had made that journey with him and so it was hardly surprising that no one else was ever going to take Linda's place.

For all his bad behaviour, Tom retains a strangely conventional side. He believes in marriage to the extent that the one woman he would not touch would be a married one. Of course, this had a great deal to do with his view of the man's position in the marriage, but even so, in his own strange way, he still valued it as an institution. After all, when he'd got his teenage girlfriend pregnant, he'd done the decent thing and walked her up the aisle. As Mary herself commented, his values are not those of the wild and amoral worlds of Vegas and Hollywood. They were shaped in working-class Wales, and that, despite everything, is where they have stayed.

And so Mary departed from the scene, Linda eventually calmed down and the whole episode became just yet another part of the Tom Jones story. But it says something for their relationship that Tom and Mary managed to stay friends despite their break-up. That is another element to Tom: it is very rare for any of his women to bad-mouth him, and a quality not often found in international stars.

But a new love was on the horizon, one that

would rock the boat even more heavily than Mary Wilson, shattering the lives of everyone involved in what would turn out to be a mess. Tom was about to meet Miss World.

CHAPTER 7

TOM AND MISS WORLD

There was no hiding the fact any more: Tom was a womaniser. Fame brings opportunities and he was only too happy to take them. There had been flings, more drawn-out affairs and one-night stands with eager and willing fans. Indeed, to accommodate all this, certain adjustments to his dressing room were needed, and so it was that he had an outer room for guests and an inner sanctum where he entertained. This, among those in the know, was called the 'workbench'.

Chris Hutchins observed that, 'He had sex, not affairs – and that was only on the road.' That was largely true, with the exception of Mary, and a few more to come, although again, there was never any question of him leaving Linda. 'Many of the women were extremely attractive,' said Chris.

'But none attractive enough to replace Linda. He always went back to her, and he always will.' These days, of course, that aspect of Tom's life has calmed down considerably, as he himself has admitted. But back then, life was one long party and he was someone who revelled in it to the extreme.

113

Despite the fairly open nature of his affairs, somehow Tom managed to get away with it, as far as the public and Linda were concerned. He was (and is) held in enormous affection by fans willing to overlook his indiscretions. Besides, with an image like his, he was bound to want something more in the evenings than to settle down with a nice cup of tea! 'Men are men,' as he once said. 'But you don't want to broadcast it; you don't want to hurt anybody.' And, in his own unique way, he tried not to. Occasionally, members of his entourage were called upon to deal with any emotional fallout, but for all Tom's carousing, he was never seen as a user. And, in his own way of thinking, he was a good husband to Linda as well. After all, he was providing her with the kind of lifestyle she couldn't have dreamed about back in the days in the Welsh valleys. She had people to look after her and she would never have to worry about money again. Clearly, he also felt he was being loyal to her, in that he had absolutely no intention of leaving her. What Linda herself thought about all this, we can only guess.

Even so, the marital boat was severely rocked from time to time and on one occasion this very nearly had an effect on Tom's career, too. The episode came about in 1974, when Tom embarked upon one of his best-known romances, with Marjorie (Marji) Wallace, who was then Miss World. This really did become a major scandal, in a way that none of the other affairs did, and the resulting fallout went on for months. On the surface, of course, it must have seemed a match made in publicist's heaven. Tom was one of the world's leading sex symbols and Miss World was, well, Miss World. What pairing could possibly be more appropriate? But, of course, that was only one side of it. In reality, Tom had a wife, Miss World had a fiancé, and there was a whole chorus of disapprovers gathering on the sidelines. It was a disaster waiting to happen and it did.

Tom first met Marji, a stunning blonde from Indianapolis, towards the end of 1973 when he was appearing at the London Palladium. Marji, who had recently been crowned Miss World, was taken backstage to meet him. Onlookers say the attraction was immediate and evident to everyone present. This was the start of a very tempestuous time. It was widely alleged that the two began seeing one another after that meeting, but at that stage, at least, it was very hush-hush and it was only later that the affair came suddenly – and disastrously – to light.

In a strange way, considering what was to follow, it almost looked as if the two wanted their affair to be out in the open. Matters, it is said, had been proceeding behind the scenes for some time when the romance was made public with pictures of the two frolicking on a beach before ending up in a passionate embrace appeared in the papers. Looking back on the events of more than thirty years ago, the whole episode almost looks as if it could have been made up, combining as it did beauty, celebrity, deceit, betrayal, glamorous locations, secret trysts and international pursuits. It was a dizzying time, but one which very nearly destroyed Marji altogether.

The pictures caused an absolute furore. Tom was

married and Marjorie had a fiancé (racing driver Peter Revson). She also went on to be linked to George Best. In those more innocent days, certain standards of behaviour were expected from Miss World. But in actual fact, Miss World didn't retain her title for much longer. Julia and Eric Morley of Mecca, who ran the competition, were incandescent with rage and took the title away from her shortly afterwards. Of course, there was a long history leading up to those pictures, although it was some time before the whole story emerged. At first Marji denied there had been any romance. 'Let me tell you the facts. Especially about the kiss that started all that fuss,' she said in a newspaper interview. 'The whole stunt – a TV spectacular featuring Tom and me on the idyllic island of Barbados – was set up jointly by the BBC and Mecca, organisers of the Miss World contest. I had met Tom once, backstage at his London show, and he struck me as an open kind of guy, genuine, pleasant and with a dynamic voice. I liked him.'

The feeling was mutual. And so the two set off to Barbados, accompanied by numerous others, including Julia Morley and Tom's entourage, and stayed at separate locations when they got to their destination. Marji takes up the story once more: 'The film was supposed to show Tom singing to me on a beautiful beach,' she said. 'And then, when he tries to make a date with me, I reply that I have to leave the island and go home. The cameras then fade out, leaving Tom to finish his song alone – just a bit of harmless fantasy. But at one point in the beach scene, Tom was supposed to lean forward and give me a sisterly kind

116

of kiss – you know, more of a peck than the real thing. Although the script had included this kiss and supposedly been checked by Mecca, this very chaste little embrace seemed to throw Julia Morley into a state of shock.'

But she wasn't the only one. The pictures were flashed around the world, while the kiss, far from chaste, looked like the full-on deal. It implied there was a great deal more going on behind the scenes than the pair was prepared to admit. Julia Morley, according to Marji, said that the pictures would be 'misconstrued' and she couldn't have been more right. And, with the double standards so often on display in the world, while the episode merely seemed to show Tom as a red-blooded man, Marji was seen as a bit of a flirt. While Linda stayed in the background, it was her mother who summed up the state of play with remarkable acuity, observing that at that time, almost every woman in the world wanted to make off with Tom Jones.

But the story wouldn't go away. A stream of women through the revolving doors of Tom's dressing room might have been one thing, but a fairly blatant relationship with a beauty queen was another. By now Tom had form. His relationship with Mary Wilson had been quite openly written about, which meant the papers felt they were able to comment at length on his new companion, too. The physical contrast between the two women added to the intrigue: Mary was dark and sultry, while Marji was an all-American blonde. At the very least it showed that Tom didn't have a particular physical type. As long as the girl was attractive, he was interested – and in this case far more than was good for any of them. But there was envy in there, as well. Not only could Tom have any woman he chose, he could also go from doe-eyed, dark-skinned women to blue-eyed blondes. It didn't seem fair, and many a male reporter chose to take a sanctimonious stance about the proceedings.

Tom was now so famous that anything with a whiff of scandal about it was utterly compelling to newspapers and public alike. And while the two couldn't have known quite what a massive story this was to be, it must be said that given the passionate nature of that kiss, neither seemed to be doing a great deal to hide what was going on. Perhaps they wanted to be found out. After all, when two people are massively attracted to each other, they tend to want to show each other off to the world and Tom and Marji may have been doing just that. But neither did they want to come completely clean at the time. Both had a great deal to lose: Tom was married, after all, while Marji was still officially Miss World. 'The truth is that that kiss was as close as Tom and I ever got – or wanted to get – throughout our week in Barbados,' said a defiant Marji in the wake of the events. 'Even if we'd wanted to have an affair, it would have been impossible. All the same, rumours of an affair between us swept London. And later on I heard the most fantastic rumour of all. According to it I had not only slept with both George Best and Tom Jones, but I'd kept a secret diary in which I'd awarded them points for "lovemanship".

'In this diary, which existed only in someone's

fertile imagination, I rated Tom Jones nine out of ten as a lover, and George Best only a poor three out of ten.' That diary element, too, kept the story in the public eye: not only was Marji seeming to have rather a racy existence, but the men in question were two of the best-known entertainers of the age. And to keep a diary! The more everyone learned, the more they wanted to know. Nor was that the end to the matter. There was another man who was also interested in Marji at the time: Engelbert Humperdinck, who shared both a manager and publicist with Tom. But shortly after meeting him, Marji went on to meet Tom, effectively cutting him out of the running.

Neither Tom nor Marji seemed capable of holding back. Neither had the slightest intention of ending the affair nor did they seem to realise the need for discretion. And, to the two of them, at least, it must have seemed such a perfect fit. Tom Jones and Miss World: the world's greatest sex symbol linked with the world's most beautiful woman. There was symmetry; it must have seemed perfect. With each utterly beguiled with the other, events quickly began to get out of hand. But underneath it all, Tom was very much behaving to form. That he was besotted with Marji was beyond doubt, but he still had every intention of returning to his marital home in due course. Almost certainly Marji didn't realise this. Although she still had a boyfriend, her love for Tom was becoming serious and when matters finally came to a crunch, she was sent into a state of shock with what could have been tragic results. Although Tom was of course affected by it all, somehow it didn't have quite the same impact on him.

As ever, it all added to the Tom Jones myth. Comparisons with the fictional character from whom he'd taken his name could not have been more apt. The fictitious character in the novel, *The History of Tom Jones* by Henry Fielding, is a spectacularly attractive womaniser, moving from one adventure to the next, while in real life Tom Jones was doing exactly the same thing. Indeed, such was the furore surrounding the affair that it was sometimes difficult to separate fact and fiction. There was certainly a giddy element to it all that didn't seem grounded in real life although the fairy tale was to shatter soon enough.

It was at this stage that George Best entered into the proceedings. Marji returned to London, leaving Tom behind in the Caribbean, and her name was promptly linked with his. Best claimed they had an affair, while Marji said he'd just been pestering her. Tom chose to believe Marji, but it is perhaps a sign that he did not take the relationship as seriously as she thought he did that he was prepared to accept her side of the story without demur. She was not, after all, his wife. With every day, the tale seemed to grow even stranger. In a bizarre turn of events, shortly after their names had been linked, Best was accused of stealing a fur coat and various other items from Marji. Ultimately he was cleared of all charges, but the ensuing publicity meant that the relationship between Tom and Marji stayed on all the front pages. Indeed, each twist and turn in the plot heightened interest. Something had to give, and it did.

More than thirty years on, it is easy to wonder at

the uproar this caused, at the time matters went from bad to worse, for Marji, at least. Angry enough about the kiss, the Morleys now heard about the diary, a story that was being circulated about town. Beside themselves, they demanded an explanation, and shortly afterwards took Marji's title away, provoking, of course, yet more press coverage and speculation about what was actually going on. The rumours, as well as reports that Marji had been unco-operative and that her boyfriend, Peter Revson, had tried to interfere, all contributed to her being stripped of her title, despite denying everything.

Indeed, in the aftermath of the event, she mounted a spirited defence of her actions. 'The Morleys sent me off to America to lie low until the Best rumpus subsided,' she said. 'But then I suddenly got a phone call telling me to come back immediately. My boyfriend, Peter Revson, was in France, racing, at the time when I phoned him. He suggested that I waited forty-eight hours, then flew to join him in France, and then we would go to London together to see the Morleys.' In retrospect this was not a wise move. The Morleys were already furious and became more so by the hour. They wanted to have it out with Marji at the earliest opportunity and made their feelings clear in no uncertain terms. 'I received a personal call from Eric Morley,' Marji related. 'It was to the point: "You can get your arse on the plane to London or you can hand in your resignation." I replied with one single word: "Charming!"'

But Marji did make her way back to London, although by now it was a little too late. 'The day after my return, a limousine came to my flat to take me to Mecca's headquarters in Southwark Street,' she recalled. 'Mrs Morley met me there and we went into her husband's office. He was sniffing indignantly and averted my gaze by staring out of the window. He had all the mannerisms of a man about to embark on a lengthy sermon. He did.' What Eric Morley went on to say had the most devastating impact on Marji's life. Up until then, despite the scandal and the furore in the press, there had been an element of game playing to the whole episode, but now the consequences of what had been going on were to become horribly real. 'We've had some bad reports of your lack of co-operation with our people on tours,' Marji remembered him saying. 'Your name has also been linked with the likes of Tom Jones and George Best. Now, on top of everything else, your boyfriend is trying to tell us what to do. In view of all this,' he intoned, 'it is my decision that you can no longer retain the title of Miss World.' Later, Marji said, 'After all the upsets and disappointments, and being organised by Mecca, I was annoyed – yet relieved – at what was now happening. I said simply, "That's fine by me."'

The former Miss World was nothing but gutsy and she put a very brave face on what must have been devastating news. For a start, she was quick to refute the Morleys' accusations that she had been unco-operative, determined to put her side of the tale. 'Honestly, there were only two occasions when I did not co-operate with the Mecca people,' she said. 'One was when I refused to have my picture taken in a cotton dress during a winter storm. And the other was when Mecca told me I could wash my hair and then minutes later when my hair was dripping wet, barged in and called me to a press conference.

'As for the episodes involving George Best and Tom Jones, there was never anything improper and if Mecca feels that these two stars are somehow tainted and not fit to meet a Miss World, then why go to such pains to get me to meet them? I'm left with the suspicion that Mecca blamed me when their publicity stunt went wrong. As for interference by Peter, that's also rubbish. He simply became fed up when I was yanked back and forth like a yo-yo.'

It was fighting stuff, but what was already a difficult situation was about to get a whole lot harder. Indeed, much worse was to come when Peter was suddenly and unexpectedly killed in a car accident in South Africa in March 1974. Marji turned to Tom for support, which he gave, and the two continued their relationship. Ultimately, however, this was the beginning of the end. A photograph brought matters to a head. Tom had been renting a house outside Las Vegas and Marji was snapped sunbathing by the pool. Here, finally, was proof that the two were, to all intents and purposes, living together, proof that finally brought the relationship to an end. Tom realised he couldn't go on any longer like this, and brought everything to a close.

No one could have predicted what would happen next. Furious, extremely upset and hurt, Marji stormed out of the house. She had lost her boyfriend, her lover and the title of Miss World, a turn of events that brought her to the point of despair. No one had expected an outcome like this, least of all Marji herself and so, in a move that stunned the world, she took an overdose, from which she mercifully made a full recovery. But as the shock of Peter's death sank in, bitterness and rows began to surface, with Marji saying, 'I don't even want to think about Tom Jones. The last year of my life has been incredible. I doubt whether there is another girl in the world who has been through what I have since I won the Miss World title. Last year things couldn't have looked better. But then everything crashed around me. I lost my title – I'm still furious about the way I was treated by Mecca when they dismissed me – and then I lost the man I loved, racing driver Peter Revson, who was killed in a terrible crash. All I can say is that this combination of events finally over-whelmed me.' Tom, incidentally, was not told about the overdose until much later on.

But she was not the only one affected by Peter's death. In the aftermath of the crash his sister Jennifer invited Marji to stay with her, only for the two women to fall out badly. Indeed, it seems to be Jennifer's realisation that a relationship had existed between Tom and Marji that incensed her, which was hardly surprising, under the cir-cumstances. And she was in no mood to keep quiet about this, providing further insight into what had been going on. 'I let Marji stay after Peter was killed in South Africa in March because she was his girlfriend and had seemed genuinely heartbroken after his death,' she said. 'She kept begging me to let her have little mementoes of my brother and finally, when they shipped his effects back from Johannesburg recently, I gave her his favourite shirt. It was the one he wore while holidaying with Marji on a Florida fishing trip. Marji hugged it and gushed her thanks.'

Their relationship, however, became enormously strained shortly afterwards, when Tom arrived in the States to play Las Vegas and contact between him and Marji was renewed. 'I got wind of the Jones thing soon after Marji came back from Indianapolis three weeks ago,' she said in a newspaper interview. 'She told me Tom Jones was a friend – just a friend, nothing more, and I believed her. I had just given her Peter's shirt and she was in happy spirits. She wanted me to meet Tom and his entourage, and a crowd of about nine or ten of us went to a restaurant in Beverly Hills for a lunch. It turned out to be a nightmare of a meal. Tom kept talking about his career and Gordon Mills, his manager, seemed mesmerised by how much money he'd made. Honestly, it was a colossal bore. They just weren't my type of people at all. I didn't want to make a scene by walking out on them, but the behaviour of some of them was so tacky. I just felt like throwing up.

'It was an absolutely degrading evening. I just kept wishing I'd not been there. Tom and Marji kept kissing each other full on the lips with arms entwined. It was quite obvious that Marji had not told me everything about her friendship with Tom. We stayed in that restaurant from lunchtime until 2am, when Marji asked me to drive her back to the house Tom had rented. When we got there I had a drink and I turned to Marji and said, "I think it's time we headed home." She gazed at me calmly and said, "You can go home but I'm staying here. Thanks for the ride and I'll see you tomorrow.'"

It was tactless of Marji, to say the least. On the one hand, no one would have expected her not to find someone else eventually, but to do so in front of Jennifer after a short space of time was perhaps a little thoughtless. Jennifer, certainly, was not amused. 'I drove home shocked,' she said. 'I was even more shocked when the next morning Marji phoned from Tom's and asked me to collect her by car from Tom's house and drive her to a manicurist's. I felt she was just using me and after this episode things between us went from bad to worse.'

This was an understatement. Jennifer's anger continued to grow as relations between the two women plummeted: clearly unaware of how her hostess felt, Marji continued to upset her. 'Marji began using my home like a hotel,' said Jennifer. 'She'd stay out overnight without telling me, and I'd leave the house unlocked because I'd have no idea if she intended coming home or not. Then she would return the following afternoon to drop off her dirty linen to my housekeeper. I kept my temper for a week or more, but finally I couldn't stand it, especially when Marji's subterfuges began to involve personal friends of mine. Once she told me she intended staying the night with some married friends of mine. Later I learned that Marji had stayed only a few minutes with them – just enough to down a drink. It was the last straw and I gave her a blast.'

It was a very unfortunate situation. Jennifer, still bereft at the loss of her brother, was clearly in a state and matters rapidly deteriorated yet further. 'My anger boiled over at seeing my brother's memory so shamed,' she said. 'It galled me to think I'd been conned by her and had actually given her Peter's beloved fishing shirt. I turned on Marji and told her what I thought of her. "You never loved Peter at all," I said. "You just used him, the way you used me, my friends and everybody else. I no longer believe anything you say and you can leave this house immediately."'

Marji, unsurprisingly, was very upset and fought back, saying that she had indeed loved Peter. 'She told me she'd led Tom on a bit in Britain and Barbados, but that nothing had happened physically,' Jennifer continued. 'But now that Peter was dead, she felt free. Those are the hard facts. That is exactly the way she explained it. Peter was dead, so forget the old and off with somebody new. That's her philosophy. I could scarcely believe my ears.

'I found myself lecturing her on the facts of life like a mother would speak to a wayward daughter. "In a few days Tom Jones will be off on another tour and you'll be dropped like a hot potato," I told her. "One day you'll probably want to marry and nobody will touch you because of your track record." Marji then lost her cool and shouted back, "Why shouldn't I go out with Tom if he wants me? I just don't care what people think. I like Tom and he likes me. That's all that matters."'

But, of course, it wasn't. For a start, Tom never had the slightest intention of leaving Linda. Secondly, Jennifer, in her grief for her brother, was not the best person to talk to about this and indeed, her anger had not let up. 'She had proved herself to be a completely selfish girl with no thought for others,' said Jennifer. 'I can't understand the mentality of someone who uses people the way she does. It's obnoxious. She even left without paying me £1,000 for clothing she had bought on my credit card. I know she's got money, because she's earned a lot recently from selling her life story. But she tries to get everything on the cheap and I've no idea if I'll ever get my money back. I've tried phoning her, but she keeps on the move, following Tom around.'

Unsurprisingly, others took a very different view: Marji's father, Dell Wallace, for a start. 'She told me Mr Jones had been a good friend to her,' he said. 'And God knows, a girl who has been through Marji's ordeal needs a friend.' And while not commenting personally, Tom also let it be known that he stood by her. 'Tom is very happy that Marji is getting better and feels that things are being said about her character when she is not in a position to defend herself,' said the ever-loyal Chris Hutchins. Nor was that actually an end to the relationship. Marji took to phoning Tom again, with the result that the two met up and the affair was back on track. But it never hit the heights it once did. Finally, as Marji began to realise that Tom would never really be hers, it fizzled out altogether. Subsequently she got together with another famous boyfriend, the tennis player Jimmy Connors, although that relationship also didn't last the course. Later she became a television host for *Good Morning Los Angeles* and

Above: Tom Jones sparring with the legendary Muhammad Ali at Deer Park, the boxer's training camp and retreat in Pennsylvania.

© *WENN/New York Daily news*

Below left: With jazz superstar Tony Bennett on *This is Tom Jones*, Tom's internationally successful television variety show that ran between 1969 and 1971.

Below right: Tom Jones doing what he does best. © *REX Features*

Above: Tom has come a long way since his Welsh roots –
pictured here with Shirley Bassey and Kenny Lynch meeting
Queen Elizabeth II at the Royal Variety Performance in 1987.

Below: Tom the family man, with his son, grandson, and
daughter-in-law in 1984.

Above left: With his son and manager Mark, who took after his father's management after his long-time manager Gordon Mills died of cancer.

Above right: Celebrating the New Year with his late mother Freda in 1989. Freda, who Tom called his 'driving force', died in 2003.

Below: In 2000 Tom Jones rocketed back into the charts with his single 'Mama Told Me Not To Come' a duet with fellow Welshman Kelly Jones of the Stereophonics. This was just one of the many successful duets which Tom Jones recorded with contemporary artists. In fact, his *Reload* album, released in 2000, became the biggest hit of his career.

A list of Tom Jones's collaborations reads like a who's who of popular artists. He is seen here performing with Stevie Wonder (*above*) and Jools Holland (*below*).

He has also made appearances with Cyndi Lauper (*above left*),
Cerys Matthews (*above right*), Robbie Williams (*bottom left*) and
Bob Geldof (*bottom right*).   © *REX Features*

Above left: In 2003 Tom Jones was the winner of the Brit Award for an Outstanding Contribution to Music. Tom rounded off the ceremony with an incredibly moving performance that he dedicated to his mum, Freda – who sadly passed away just two weeks before the show. © *REX Features*

Above right: Arise Sir Tom Jones. © *REX Features*

Below: With the Beverley Sisters at the Investitures Ceremony, March 2006. The Beverley sisters seem somewhat overwhelmed by the fact that they have been honoured MBEs, met Her Majesty, and hugged Tom Jones all in one day. © *REX Features*

Above: Tom attracted a huge crowd on London's Southbank when he went busking for charity on BBC2's *The Culture Show* in 2008.

Below: Performing at a Help for Heroes concert at Twickenham in 2010.

Above: Alongside Tom's fellow original cast members of *The Voice*, (*from left*) Danny O'Donoghue, Jessie J and will i am.

Below left: Appearing beside the very best of British artists, Tom was honoured to be asked to perform at the Queen's Diamond Jubilee concert.

Below right: Still doing what he does best – thrilling his adoring fans with his incredible voice.

All photos © Rex Features

Entertainment Tonight.

As for Tom, it was business as usual. He'd had a narrow escape, but that wasn't going to put him off his stride. Indeed, his career was changing shape. Throughout the 1970s he was nearly a permanent fixture in Las Vegas, a time in his career that he was later to describe as being a little flat. While he was as popular as ever, he was not dominating the charts in the way he had done in the sixties and at times, he must have wondered if he would ever do so again. In fact, his longevity as a performer has been quite extraordinary, but back then, settled into the world's premiere entertainment location amid the hot, dusty sands of the Arizona desert, he was content to let matters ride.

CHAPTER 8

JONES, THE WEALTH

By the turn of the seventies, Tom was an enormously rich man. But this was a Britain in which the rich were being taxed until the pips squeaked, and once Tom became one of them this was not a place where he wanted to live. He uprooted to Los Angeles shortly afterwards, where he bought a house that had once belonged to the singer Dean Martin for $1 million (£500,000). Under the regime of those days, he was unable to return to the UK without facing a colossal tax bill. The move was a permanent one, with Tom acquiring a green card and shipping his by then rather splendid collection of furniture overseas. While he expressed mixed views about the move, it was certainly necessary to protect his fortune but it caused him a certain amount of anguish, too. 'I love Britain and I love living there,' he said. 'It's home. But I've been forced into exile and I don't like it one little bit.'

The move made sense for other reasons, too. Throughout the seventies, Tom's career was based very solidly in the States, especially Las Vegas. He was content to take up an almost permanent residence in the world's greatest playground, staying in a suite stretching over two floors in Caesar's Palace Hotel. When he moved to LA on a permanent basis, he took his parents, his sister Sheila and her family with him, but it was now that Linda really entered her reclusive phase. She settled into the Bel Air mansion and from then on, was content to stay at home while Tom and the rest of the family caroused in Las Vegas. Whether she was happy, only she can say. She still had her Tommy Woodward, while the rest of the world had Tom Jones. Not that Tom was a bad husband, by any means. Chris Hutchins recalled that in the sixties, he had given Linda a ring that had cost £12,000, an absolute fortune back then.

The seventies, however, were to prove a slight lull in Tom's career. He continued to release singles – 'Daughter of Darkness', 'She's a Lady', 'Till' and 'The New Mexican Puppeteer' among others – and finally, in 1977, 'Say You'll Stay Until Tomorrow', which was to be his last hit for a decade. But in some quarters he was now regarded as yesterday's man. There was a further blow in 1977 when his good friend Elvis Presley died. Tom was devastated.

Not only did he miss Elvis's friendship, but he also must have missed that link back to the earliest years, when he was just starting out. And, if truth be told, what happened to Elvis is an awful warning as to what can happen when a showbusiness career goes wrong. Bloated and out of touch, Elvis was in a sorry state when he died, which must have been a painful sight for his close friends, including Tom. It was a sad time for all concerned.

But the world was changing, and so was the music. Punk was beginning to gain ground and crooners like Tom were no longer at the forefront of musical happening. It was not, as he said himself, a particularly fruitful time in his career, but neither was life difficult. He was enjoying his fame and his wealth, and was generous with it, especially to his family. As the seventies moved into the eighties, Tom's family life was also changing. In 1981, Tom Senior passed away, an event that hit his son hard. The cause was emphysema, brought on by cigarettes and the hard life of a miner. Then Tom's son Mark got married, and in 1983, made his father a granddad to little baby Alexander at the age of just forty-three. As time went on, Tom became more careful about looking after himself. Now practically living in Las Vegas, where he did two shows a night, his day was an unusual one: he would rise mid to late afternoon, having retired well into the early hours, but was then meticulous about keeping himself fit. He and Mark would make full use of the gym at Caesar's Palace: they played heavily competitive games of racquetball against one another. Tom had also cut back on the booze. 'I don't abuse myself any longer,' he said. 'I don't touch alcohol in Vegas: it's too easy for the voice to go.' He was careful about what he ate, too, although in today's terms it might be considered a little unhealthy. 'I have it every day,' he said. 'Steak, sometimes ham, and eggs, scrambled or poached. I can be a gourmet anytime. What I need here is protein. I regularly sweat off two pounds during a show. You have to give something back to the body.'

When he wasn't in Vegas, Tom continued his life as a *bon viveur*, but remained extremely careful about how he treated his body. 'I've never got into drugs, but I've always enjoyed a drink,' he said. 'When I was a boy, my father and uncles would go into the pub and I wanted to stand alongside them. The idea was to consume a lot of beer and not show it. Drugs are completely the opposite, people take drugs for oblivion. I had a bass player who used to like a drink and however much he had, you could prop him against a pillar and he'd carry on playing. But one evening he tried hashish and when he got on stage he just couldn't function. I like to drink but I leave it till night time, till after the show. I'll have wine with dinner, then cognac, end up with champagne.'

By this stage in his career, Tom had reaped huge benefits from a lifetime of success. He had by now sold about 50 million records, and was an extremely rich man. He might not touch alcohol in Vegas, but he did elsewhere: apart from champagne, he was now an expert on fine wine. And

132

while he might no longer have been top of the pops, his popularity among female fans was undiminished. 'It's very sexy and aimed at women,' he said of his show, and women, indeed, lapped it up. Knickers continued to rain down on the stage, as did the occasional hotel room key. It was not unknown for women to rip off their blouses in his presence, too. Tom played up to it all, wiping his chest with the lingerie before handing it back to its overexcited owner, all the while dressing in ever tighter clothing, more often than not open to the waist.

'I know that is one thing that appeals to women,' he said. 'When women get excited, it gives me a good feeling. I've been wearing tight pants for years. They are part of my performance. They are successful. Why should I stop wearing them?' Why indeed? He was enjoying himself and earning a fortune in the process. His life was a world away from the poverty in which he had started out, and he had his family, apart from Linda, around him to share it with. Mark had officially joined the entourage: he now worked for his father as his assistant, good preparation for the role he was ultimately to assume.

And he was enormously good natured about events that could have floored a less experienced performer. On one occasion, he related that a woman rushed on to the Las Vegas stage when he was mid-song. Ever the professional, he stopped: 'I said, "What's your name? Where do you come from? Are you married?" he recalled 'She said, "Yes." I said, "Oh no, where's he sitting?" And then he came up and joined her onstage and I felt

133

in a bit of a spot. I thought he'd be angry or embarrassed. I said, "Please sir, I don't want to get you upset about your wife or anything..." And he started laughing. Then he said, as his wife became more and more demonstrative towards me, "Don't worry about it, Tom. You pump up the tyres and I'll ride the bike!" It was hard not to be won over by such a jovial attitude to life.'

Despite the fact that his life was now so bound up in the States, however, Tom had not forgotten his roots. And so, in 1983, he made plans to tour Britain for the first time in a decade, something he knew was a bit of a risk. Although he had been releasing albums which had continued to sell well, it was years since he'd had a hit single, and so there was a real chance he might have been forgotten, or at least, gone downhill. But Tom was determined to prove himself once more. 'The fans from ten years or more ago will be expecting me to be at least as good as I was then, if not better, and the new people – of which I hope there will be a good proportion – will only know what they've heard,' he said. 'So I've got to knock them out. I can't wait.'

He was deadly serious in his undertaking and, in the background, there was still Gordon Mills taking a firm hand in running Tom's career. 'Live performances and recording are his whole life,' he said. 'Money just isn't the issue. If he suddenly dropped in favour and his money halved, he would still work as much as he does. It's doing something and achieving, rather than saying, "How much am I getting for it?" [He's] getting really wound up [about the new tour.] He's a true Gemini. Never emotional off stage, more emotional on stage. He doesn't have a big ego.' Had he, Gordon was asked, ever seen Tom cry? 'Yes – one night when we got very drunk and we cried on each other's shoulder. But he never shows his feelings off stage like he does when he's on.'

As the tour dates neared, Tom was keen to emphasise that he was still as British as he had ever been. 'I used to say to Gordon, "I'd like to go back to Britain,"' he said. 'And he'd say, "As soon as we can work it out, I will." And time just kept going on. Thank God we can finally do it. I still feel British and not American. I'm a Welshman abroad. I've not become an American citizen. I'm a resident of America with a British passport. So although I'm away from Britain physically, I've never mentally stopped thinking about it and mixing with British people.'

It would seem that despite all the luxury on offer, Tom still suffered from the odd twang of homesickness – and in particular for that most British of institutions: the pub. 'That's what I'm homesick for more than anything,' said Tom. 'The British pub. When I lived in England I used to pop into the local – the Anchor at Shepperton – for a pint as a break. You can't do that here. There's the Bel Air Hotel down the road from me and I go down there in the afternoon, but there's nobody at the bar! If there is anyone there, they just sit there.'

And then, of course, there was the act itself. For over twenty years now Tom had been a professional performer and had honed his performances into what appeared to be a direct and very sexy flirtation with each and every woman in the

135

audience. About 80 per cent of his audiences tended to be women, although he did like to have some men there as well – 'enough men in the audience to make it interesting ... they usually give off good vibes and are never negative, even though they know what my act is all about.'

They knew all right, and so did everyone else. Tom was born a ladies' man, and the circumstances of his astonishing life had now turned him into a seducer par excellence. 'Most songs I do on stage have something to do with man/woman relationships,' he said. 'When I first went on stage at sixteen in a pub, I'd just grab hold of the microphone and sing. I wanted to get the sound right, to get what I had to say across.

'Then, when that became more natural, I thought I had to put something extra in. So I started to dance along with the uptempo things – and it got reactions. And I did more and more. With ballads, too, I started to try to express not just vocally but physically, with hand and body movements. Some people say they can put their mind elsewhere [when performing] and just do it naturally. I think about all the words and every movement that I perform. I really get inside a song.'

He wasn't the only one. Women adored it, each feeling that he was singing (and gyrating) especially for them. But, asked if he picked a special person to sing to each night, Tom was unequivocal. 'No, I don't,' he said, 'because most of the time the spotlights are on me and I can't really see the audience. The first time I did a matinée in the open air, the audience was there, looking at me and it was a strange feeling. At nights, I can generally see only the first and second rows, unless someone comes to the stage. But generally, I feel an audience, even if I can't actually see them. I do try to catch eyes and I look out for people rather than into the blackness, but not just one particular person because all the people in that audience are there to see me. I'm singing to them all, not just one.'

Tom was also questioned about his motivation at that stage. After all, by that time he was an extremely rich man, one who would never have to work again if he didn't want to. So, what made him continue to go through the slog of getting out there on stage? 'I still have exactly the same needs as a performer,' he said. 'I have to prove every time I step on stage that I'm as good as ever and that proof keeps me going. I have to give 100 per cent of myself each time I step on stage. I have to be able to say after every show, "Yes, I've done it again."

'The only good thing about earning a lot of money is that it means you haven't any need to think about it. For me, it's like getting paid for a hobby, anyway. In Wales I worked in construction during the day and sang in pubs at night – for no money. Maybe I'd get some drinks free when I first started. Then I began getting paid at the working men's clubs. And it went from there. Some people have interests in other areas. I have none. Performing is my life and I'll carry on until I can physically do it no more.' In the event the tour was a great success.

In 1986, there was a very abrupt shock for Tom, one that hit him hard, both on a personal and professional level. In July of that year, Gordon Mills died suddenly and unexpectedly of cancer, when he was still only in his fifties. The blow to Tom was enormous. Gordon had taken him from the clubs and pubs of the Welsh valleys to become one of the most famous singing stars in the world and he was well aware of what he owed his old friend. And that was another reason to grieve: the two men were friends, not just business associates. They had worked together now for more than twenty years and his sudden departure from the stage left Tom at a loss, for once and very unusually, unable to hide his grief. 'I like a certain amount of formality and discipline, you have to have it in order to survive,' he said, some years afterwards. 'The last time I cried was when my manager died, I couldn't control myself and I don't like getting out of control.'

In the event, despite his personal grief, his career actually went on to achieve new heights. For a start, 'It's Not Unusual' was re-released as a tribute to Gordon, and took Tom once more to the top of the charts in May 1987. Then, Tom's son Mark stepped into the breach and took over as his father's manager. He had, after all, been working as Tom's assistant for some years now, and knew the trade as well as anyone, having been practically born into it and having watched his famous father at close hand throughout his life. This was to give Tom a new lease of life and Mark remains his manager to this day.

Indeed, Tom's relationship with his son had

always been a close one, despite the months and years he spent on tour. 'Mark knows me better than anybody,' said Tom in the late eighties. 'I've often asked him if it's difficult being my son, but he's got a strong personality of his own and I've only wanted whatever made him happy. When he was sixteen, I was travelling a lot, wasn't seeing him much. I got home, we were out to dinner one night, I could see he was moody and I asked him what the matter was. He said he wanted me to be with him more. I talked to his headmaster and he said, "Let him leave school and take him on tour with you." He's been with me ever since and after Gordon Mills died last year, he became my manager and now he's really come into his own.'

It was a touching observation and one that displayed a side of Tom the public didn't normally see: that he was a really good father and, for all his faults, a warm family man... His relationship with his son speaks volumes. The fact that Mark – a hard-working, conventional young man, who has never displayed any of Tom's womanising tendencies and by this time was about to make him a grandfather for the second time – chose to stay close to his father is something of which he can justly be proud.

Tom, of course, was a very young grandfather, but even so, it must have brought it home to him that he was no longer the youthful idol of yesteryear. Rather, he was a mature man, in actual fact far more attractive than he had been in his younger days, but getting older, nonetheless. He was aware of the passing of the years and determined to keep himself in shape. 'I don't feel old and I don't think I'm old,' he said. 'I'm fitter than I ever was as a young man. Now I work out, run every day. I'm in peak condition.'

Although he remained based in the United States, Tom now began to return to the UK more frequently, continuing to tour and catch up with his British fans. His personal life continued to intrigue the public, too. Linda remained in the Bel Air home, which by the late eighties was worth about £10 million, surrounded by the trappings of luxury, none of which seemed to interest her. Tom acknowledged that, and the unusual nature of their relationship, too. 'She's a misfit,' he said. 'A lot of women would love to have the money and all the socialising, but it doesn't do a lot for her. She doesn't like travelling, she can't stand crowds, she is a bit agoraphobic.

'If she does go out, she has to get some Dutch courage. In order to go anywhere, she has a drink. She doesn't like to go to parties because she says, "I'll only have a few drinks to give me confidence and then I'll make a fool of myself." My life just goes against the grain for her. What she'd really like would be for me to have a nine-to-five job and she'd rather be in Britain. She misses seeing her sister, but she won't travel on her own and being married keeps me single.

'If it hadn't been for my wife, I'd have been married five or six times now. I've weighed it all up and I don't think there's anything with more advantages. If we separated, I wouldn't be any better off and she's never said she wanted to leave me, so why change? She accepts I'll have affairs, although she doesn't go along with it, she doesn't

140

say, "Oh, it's all right." She just tells me, "Be careful." I've never wanted to have affairs, they just happened; it's better if they don't.'

He was also adamant that he never led any of the other women on. 'I'm always honest about the fact that I'm married and it's never going to change,' he said. 'It's putting your cards on the table before you play the game. I've always been aware of my attraction, I can't remember not being aware. My wife really wants me there with her, but I'm away touring a lot. When I am home, I reassure her by doing all the right things: I talk to her, I listen. I think she's as happy as she can be, I've never asked her. She knows her limitations. She's not a very confident person.'

It was brutal, but about as honest an assessment of the relationship between the two of them as he could possibly have made. The facts were laid bare: he was going to have affairs and Linda could either accept that and stay, or decide to go. Clearly Linda decided to stay. And who is to say that she wasn't happy? Other women may have had Tom for days, weeks or even months, but no one other than Linda had him for a lifetime. He had never left her, never married anyone else. To the world he was Tom Jones, but with Linda he was still Tommy Woodward, the name, incidentally, he was knighted by. As the song had it, he was always faithful to her in his fashion. It was just not a fidelity that precluded other friends.

'We've been together for thirty years now, Linda and me, and the secret is simple,' he said. 'It's successful because we will never split, no matter what. Linda knows what I get up to, but she just says, "OK, you be careful and don't go runnin' off with some young girl." So I say, not me, I won't, not ever because for me Linda is like my right arm. It still doesn't stop me from finding other women attractive, though... She's often threatened to go, but as she says – go where? She'd rather be with me than without me. You see, we married at sixteen, very young, very much in love. You don't forget that. And of course, she enjoys the rewards that my work has brought.'

Tom's interesting attitude to fidelity aside there were other elements to the marriage both had to contend with and have overcome. It frequently happens that when a couple from a poor background get married and the man becomes successful, he rises to the challenge of the new way of life and his partner doesn't. That is exactly what happened here. The difference is that in very many cases, the husband trades in his first wife for someone he sees as befitting his new status, whereas for all his philandering, Tom has never done that. But the couple did find that they now had wildly differing attitudes to their circumstances and it says something for the strength of the relationship that it still endured.

'I must say, she's never adapted to the Hollywood lifestyle, loathes parties, leaving the house, meeting people,' said Tom, in an interview in the late eighties. 'I'll give you this example. We were house hunting recently and I went to look at a house belonging to Bob Evans, the famous film producer. Of course, Linda came along with me then, because she wanted to see the house. Nice house, lovely, but we wanted something a bit more modern, newer. So we looked around, then he said, why don't we stay, he was screening a movie in his private cinema. We said sure, great, then in walked Jack Nicholson and his girlfriend. Well, Linda was OK, we got along fine.

'But if I'd said, let's go to Bob Evans's house, meet Jack Nicholson and his girl, it would have been, "Not me, not me." If she ever wants to go out, it's to the little restaurant round the corner. I say fine. See, I play her game, too. I don't force her out on to the Hollywood scene. If she's happy to be the woman at home, suits me, because at home she's the boss. That's just the way I like it. Gives you something to come home to, somewhere you can relax.'

Nor had his views about the role of women changed from the early days. 'The man should be the provider,' he said, 'and the husband should make the decisions. I think women are happier that way, they really like to lean on a man, to depend on him. Look at history, at men in war. If they're real men they stand up and defend; when necessary they'll give up their lives for what they believe in.' It may not have been progressive thinking, but it suited Tom's image down to the ground. He was, after all, originally a bit of rough from the valleys in Wales, and despite the fact that he had now become a world-class sophisticate, that ruggedness still lurked below the surface. Declarations like that did his image no harm at all.

And he continued to revel in his undoubted sex appeal, as potent on-stage as it was off. 'I always try and look for sensual, sexual songs that move people,' he said. 'I don't want it just to be nice. I

143

want the audience to experience something, to think about the relationship between a man and a woman because that's what makes the world go round. I go on in a tuxedo then the tie comes off, then the jacket. It's like foreplay in sex rather than just jumping on somebody. I've learnt what works by trial and error.'

'I took my tie off one night just to give myself more freedom and the women got excited, so now I always do it,' he continued. 'I perspire a lot, I used to be a bit self-conscious about it, but women handed me their hankies to wipe my brow and then they wanted them back, so that's become part of the act. And I always wear tight trousers rather than loose ones and it seems to work. I change the act every January, the people who regularly come to see me wonder if it's going to be as good, but they always say, "It's better than ever."' Modest, it wasn't, but Tom retained the appeal that had made him famous a good two decades before.

He also retained the ambition. His reappearance in his native land had paid off. As well as being one of the most famous performers in the United States, he had now cultivated a whole new generation of fans back home. Indeed, it was just adding to his list of admirers, for he retained the fans of yesteryear when he was just starting out, and now there was the new blood who were discovering him for the first time. He was thrilled, and made no secret of it, either.

'Retire?' he once barked. 'Not me! I'm too ambitious and I still want the hits. I want to be back up there at the top of the charts once again. There's a younger element coming to my shows now and buying the records, which is great. Means I can still cut it, still got the edge. It's all part of the game, isn't it? Dressing up, acting the part, having your picture taken. It's good business, lets people see what you're really like, reminds them you're still around. No point in staying too aloof – makes you look as if you've got something to hide.'

But there wasn't much chance of that. His image was more in your face than ever: the trousers even tighter, the tan darker, that full-wattage smile melting everyone around him. His behaviour could be outrageous. It is said that on one occasion he sent a female who came to interview him packing because she wasn't attractive enough, but somehow, he managed to get away with it. Perhaps it was because he combined genuine and breathtaking sex appeal with a certain amount of self-deprecation; never did he seem to be taking himself too seriously. 'Me a poser? Of course I am!' he declared to one interviewer. 'I'm posing for you.'

Above all, he continued to thrill as an entertainer. 'You can't match the feeling of being on stage in front of a responsive audience to anything else. Well, almost anything. Know what I mean?' It was hard not to. In recent years he's played it down, but back in the eighties, Tom was happy to admit that he was more than prone to straying from the green, green grass of home. 'Yes, I'm a sexy guy,' he remarked to a pretty girl who was sent to interview him. 'I feel sexy. Not just now and again; it's more of an awareness. I mean, I'm a man and I'm aware that you're a good-looking woman sitting next to me. That's a sexual situation, an energy. There's a definite charge.'

How could any woman resist that? Tom was such a shameless flirt, on-stage and off, women simply couldn't help themselves and they fell for him in their droves. A stage strewn with knickers remained his hallmark. 'Not just in a place like Vegas, either, where everyone is out to have a wild time,' he commented. 'It happens in England, too. Depends what the English woman is doing at the time. In the right situation, any woman can relax, let herself go.' Vintage Tom, and there was a great deal more yet to come.

CHAPTER 9

KISS

While there has never been any question of Tom and Linda splitting up, by the late eighties and into the nineties, they were living lives that were even more separate from one another than ever before. Linda had returned to Wales, and stayed there for a year, seemingly tired of her life in LA, where the couple had also recently sold their old house. They had bought a new one, but even so, it seemed that she had finally had enough of the life she shared with Tom and wanted to return to all that was familiar.

It is the closest the marriage has ever come to a split and in retrospect perhaps it was a good move for her to make in terms of deciding what she wanted to do. Would she stay with Tom, the man she loved, but whose affairs she would have to tolerate? Or would she decide that it was just not worth it and that she was going to return to her original home. What to do? Linda probably wasn't entirely clear what she wanted herself – or rather, she knew perfectly well what she wanted. It was a faithful Tom, based in Wales. But that, alas, was not an option open to her and so instead she had to decide which of the available outcomes was the one she wanted to pursue. After all, money was no object. It was entirely possible for the two to run separate establishments on either side of the world and, given the amount of time he spent on the road, Tom could hardly complain if Linda, just for once, wanted to do her own thing. And so, for a short time, she did.

Tom took this with his usual *laissez faire* attitude. 'Well, she likes being in Wales,' he said. 'She's very fussy in the house. She's doing up the house the way she wants it. She's done everything she wants to the house in Los Angeles. And she won't travel by herself. One time she would, but now she won't. But she is coming back to LA. Or at least, she says she is. She has to come back because we live there.'

And, of course, ultimately, she did. As she came to realise, staying in Wales would have meant leaving Tom, who was clearly going to remain based in the States, and Linda simply didn't want to do that. She spent about a year on her own be-fore deciding to return to LA, but she clearly had some tough decisions to make. Again, would she continue as she had been doing, turn a blind eye to Tom's numerous dalliances and go back to her old life? Or would she break away from the life she had lived for so long, the husband she still clearly adored, and then return to Wales? It was inevitable that she would finally return to Tom. By this time, she had simply given up too much to throw it all away. Many years earlier she must have accepted that if she was to stay married to Tom, then that marriage was going to be an unusual one, but it is not one that she has ever wanted to end.

And what is so easy to overlook is that the bond between the two of them was very strong. For the marriage simply to have survived as long as it had done, given Tom's dalliances and Linda's shyness, meant that it had grown in strength. No other women, not even Miss World, had been able to usurp her in his affections, while in Tom, she still saw her old childhood sweetheart, Tommy Woodward. And he was still there, behind it all. International singing star or not, Tom was still the boy from the valleys in Wales. But the relationship between the two continued to cause as much speculation as ever. People simply could not understand Linda's decision to stay. She was acting in a way totally at odds with modern ideas about women and their husbands. Also much commented on was how incredibly rarely Linda ever said a word to explain her own attitude to what was going on.

But just as there were by now two Toms, so, too, there were two sides to Linda, for she was not quiet at home. In her rare public appearances, of course, she cut a reclusive figure, one who never spoke and was totally dominated by her husband. In private, however, just as the old Tommy Woodward still existed, so, too, did the old fiery Linda. She gave as good as she got in their life together at home, and while she might rarely utter a word in the outside world, at home, in her own territory, she could hold her own. Tom might have got away with more than most husbands, but when Linda finally had enough, she let him know it. It was not absolute calm when the two were behind closed doors.

Friends and relatives tried to explain this dichotomy in Linda's character, pointing out that there was far more to her than merely the image of the retiring wife. 'She has always stayed in the background,' said Tom's cousin, Idris Jones. 'She is a nice lady. I don't say she's shy when she's amongst her family but I don't think she likes the limelight. Tom and her are very close. When you see them together, they will have a laugh. We have sat down many a time to have a meal with them. I think she has an artistic eye and likes to see things looking nice. She likes seeing that the house is decorated all right and it's a lovely house. A maid comes in every day. That's the way she likes it. She enjoys the home and loves to have her family at her house. She makes you feel at home and is always pleased to see you. I have always enjoyed our stays.'

As far as the experiment with living in Wales was concerned, her friends and family tried to explain that, too. It was a way of allowing Linda to get a breath of air and, perhaps, time off from being Mrs Tom Jones; it was to allow her to reconnect with her life, and to make decisions about what she really wanted to do. And it was, perhaps, a way of coping with empty-nest syndrome. Mark, after all, spent most of the year on tour with his father and so, with both husband and son globetrotting, it was hardly surprising that Linda decided that she, too, wanted to do her own thing.

'She wanted to come back to Wales to live,' said Tom's cousin Dorothy Woodward. 'Tom bought her a house there. Tom was doing his tours but he'd come back there. But it didn't work out. They had a beautiful home in Los Angeles – which Nicholas Cage bought off them. It had previously been Dean Martin's house but they sold it because Linda thought she wanted a view overlooking the hills and so Tom bought her a house looking over the San Fernando Valley, where we have stayed. I would say she misses Wales, but there again she had the house here. She wasn't mixing enough. I suppose after being so long in your own company, and just with people who work for you, it's difficult.'

The Welsh estate did have one benefit, though: it was an ideal place to entertain grandchildren. 'I used to own a house in Cowbridge in Wales with forty-four acres,' said Tom. 'One day, when my grandson was about nine, he wanted to buy some air rifles and I said: "OK, let's go into Cardiff to buy them." He didn't get bored with it like some kids would have done. He stuck at it and he's done very well.' He did indeed, so much so that ultimately he turned world competitor in the sport.

But still Linda's patience was being pushed to

the full. Tom's philandering was as full on as ever, but this time round something happened that had never come about before – one of his frequent affairs resulted in the birth of a child. The affair became public knowledge when the baby was born. He had been involved with Katherine Berkery, a model, and when she became pregnant, a DNA test after her son was born showed that it was 99.7 per cent likely that Tom was the father.

Tom has never met his son, nor publicly acknowledged him, but he has made financial provision for him. Linda chose not even to acknowledge what had happened. Indeed, while still in her nightie, she flung open the windows of the house in Cardiff to address a group of waiting journalists: 'Tom has told me he was never with her and I believe him,' she said. Even so, for the first time ever in the Jones's marriage, rumours began to circulate to the effect that a divorce could be on the cards. This might have had no grounding in reality and could simply be the product of journalists imagining what they themselves would do if they were in Linda's shoes, but if ever there was a time when Tom had pushed his luck to the limits, this was it.

He and Katherine had actually met back in 1987, at Regines nightclub in New York. The two had dinner the following night after one of Tom's shows and almost immediately became inseparable, a state of affairs that lasted for about four days. With that, Tom was off on the road again, and was reportedly less than delighted when it emerged that Katherine was carrying his child. 'I knew Tom was the father,' she said. 'I hadn't slept with anyone since him. I didn't know what to do, I couldn't tell my family or friends. I had always dreamed of having a baby and a husband and a cottage.'

It was a sad situation, not least for Jonathan, Tom's son. There is a strong physical resemblance between the two, and yet they have never had any contact. Years later, Katherine spoke about the hurt. 'I have told Jonathan about Tom,' she said. 'We have watched his videos together. When he was younger he asked about him a lot, but he doesn't seem to any more. He thinks Tom is a good guy and I would never say anything to turn him against him. He has no clue he's been rejected. It's been hard for me to know what to say. One day Jonathan will find out the truth, but I won't say a negative thing about Tom. He's not old enough yet to understand. I have never lied to Jonathan, but I have hidden the truth. I don't think he needs me to tell him – one day he'll work it out for himself.'

Jonathan, sadly, brought out a harsh streak in Tom's character, however. He has often spoken about how much he would like to meet his father, but there is very little chance that he will ever do so, unless Tom experiences a complete change of heart. It is one of the few subjects he is unwilling to talk about at length with interviewers, and when he has done, it's been to talk about the difference between having a baby with his wife and someone else. 'I deny the child is mine because the test is not 100 per cent,' he once said. 'He wasn't formed out of love for somebody. It was an accident, but financially he's taken care of.'

The great irony is that not only does Jonathan resemble Tom – 'I can see the likeness in the boy to his father,' said Katherine. 'There's something about his chin and his hazel eyes' – but he also appears to have his singing voice and charisma. 'He did not have to be taught,' said Katherine, when he was eleven. 'He's just doing what comes naturally and he enjoys it so much. He can be shy, but not when it comes to singing a song. He has always been crazy about music. Someone watching him said to me: "He has star power. There's something about him. He has a maturity way beyond his years." The girls just love him. I think it's because he's quite shy and cool. He's also a gentleman. A lot of boys his age go from one girl to another, changing their minds every twenty-four hours, but Jonathan is not like that. He stays with them for quite a long time.' Unlike, she scarcely needed to add, his dad.

As for Jonathan himself, he has accepted the situation with remarkable good grace. He launched a singing career and did some modelling. Unsurprisingly, given his parentage, he has turned into a handsome boy. But he has not bad-mouthed his father: apart from repeating a desire that the two could one day meet, he has never given into the temptation to criticise. He is a credit to his mother and one can only hope that one day he gets his much-cherished wish to meet his dad.

By the late eighties, it was time for a total rethink when it came to Tom's career. The fact that he never needed to work again in this life and a dozen others being immaterial, as he himself has so often remarked, performing is his life. He might not have to do it, but he still wants to do it, and that has never changed. But what had to change was his style. For the best part of two decades he had been performing in much the same way and there was no escaping it: his act looked dated and a whole new approach was needed.

That approach came from none other than his son Mark. Now Tom's manager, and proving very successful at the job, Mark was able to take a step back and decide on the changes that would have to be made. First and foremost was the knicker issue. It had become such a big part of the act that critics were forgetting anything else going and tending to judge how well everything had gone by the number of knickers that landed on stage. What had started out as proof that Tom was the sexiest man alive had become an unwelcome distraction and one that was appearing dated at that, as Mark suggested.

'He pointed out problems with my show that I would never have been aware of,' said Tom. 'For instance, I never saw that the underwear thing was having a terrible effect. The critics had stopped paying any attention to my music. They wouldn't even mention my voice; they were just looking at what was happening with the women. My son told me, "We can't stop the underwear thing but don't pick them up and wipe your face with them. Concentrate on the music." He also suggested that I stop wearing my trousers so tight.'

The change to the act worked wonders, while in no way depriving Tom of his sex-symbol image: now he just appeared to be a slightly more mature figure, rising loftily above the lingerie as it rained down upon the stage. Nor did his decision to stop picking up underwear make women stop throwing it at him. But now the knickers landing on stage were not so much a sign of lust as affection. He had moved on.

The next item to address was the music itself. His old hits – 'Delilah', 'The Green, Green Grass of Home', 'What's New Pussycat?', *et al* – were as popular as ever when he sang them on stage, but if he was going to continue releasing singles, he had to come at it from a whole new angle. A more modern direction was needed.

And so, Tom set out to experiment, with varying degrees of success. There had been a brief flirtation with Disco, probably best forgotten about, but much more positive was a move towards singing in a musical. In a studio recording Tom sang the role of El Cordobes in *Matador* with a view to the musical making it on to the West End stage. While that never materialised, it lead to a massive hit in spring 1987 in the form of the ballad, 'A Boy from Nowhere', which many people took to be his own story and it was proof that he still had the potential for massive chart success.

Even so, he still needed to come up with something brand new. In showbiz circles the secret of success is endless reinvention – look at Madonna – and it was felt that it was not enough for Tom simply to continue as he had been doing. And so everyone on the team looked for some inspiration as to what to do next. It was found in the most unlikely area possible, with the diminutive singer Prince. Back in the eighties, Prince had had a huge hit with the song 'Kiss', but no one dreamed it might be an idea for Tom to follow suit, although he did, with enormous success. As with so much else in his life, it really came about by chance. 'Well, I was doing "Kiss" live on stage and not really thinking about recording it because Prince had already had a big hit with it,' said Tom in a 1999 interview. 'But then, when I did it on television on the Jonathan Ross Show, The Art of Noise saw me doing it and asked, would I record it with them for an album they were putting out? And I said, sure, you know, thinking it was going to be an album track. But when we listened to the finished thing, we all agreed that it sounded like a single. So we put it out, and that is what got me back on Top 40 radio again, worldwide. I had already had a hit the year before with "A Boy from Nowhere", but worldwide "Kiss" was the one that got me back on Top 40 radio and got me on MTV. We did a video for it and I won an award that year, on MTV which was something I hadn't done before. So I was back on track again.'

That was putting it mildly: 'Kiss' was a phenomenal success and opened up a whole new phase in Tom's career. Indeed, he was now singing to a whole new audience. He might have been old enough to be their father, but a new generation was responding to him just as eagerly as their parents did twenty years earlier. More than that, he became hip. Not only did the younger crowd like him, but it was fashionable to like him, too. It was a development that has affected no other star of his age or generation: somehow he managed to stay that crucial step ahead.

He was in no doubt as to who should take the

credit for his newly revived career. Mark was turning out to be a superb manager – a position he holds to this day – and his new way of looking at Tom's career and fresh input was working incredibly well. 'It's unusual being managed by your son but he made me more aware of things, like when I did Prince's "Kiss",' said Tom. 'I had a lot of input with Wyclef [Jean], but Mark was instrumental in getting us together. I'm thrilled, and he brought out another side of me. I could easily just do a retrospective tour and bang out the classics for the rest of my life but I want to do something new.

'The seventies was a bad patch for me musically but the classics carried me through the years. My public image wasn't great; it was all retro. This has been a bit of a rebirth for me. I want to make contemporary records. There aren't many people of my generation who can sell records any more. Paul McCartney struggled and so did Mick Jagger with his solo album yet the Stones can sell out on tour. That's a nostalgia thing and I'm not cashing in on that, although I'll still do "Delilah" live. You shouldn't alienate your hardcore fans. I would be bored if I retired – I haven't got any hobbies. I've never played golf, my attention span is too short, so I have to sing. I get impatient, I suppose it's quite childish really. I'll carry on until my voice doesn't work. I love that I can still get the power.'

He certainly could. Even so, not everything worked out to his advantage. In 1991 he worked on an album called *Carrying A Torch* with Van Morrison, but it was not a great commercial success. He also recorded an R&B album that was never released. Much more successful, and canny, however, was the re-release of 'It's Not Unusual', which had the enormous advantage of reminding all his older fans of their youth, while demonstrating to younger people that the old songs could still cut it.

By now it was clear that Mark was a quite exceptional manager and in that Tom has been extremely lucky. It is very unusual for an entertainer of his longevity to have only been managed by two people throughout his entire career. The strength of the relationships, first with Gordon and then with Mark, meant that he was able to put his complete trust and faith in people who were looking after his interests. It freed him up to do what he did best – perform – and meant there were no gnawing anxieties in the background as to how it was all going to work out. Mark was doing a brilliant job, not least in making his father proud.

In the early nineties, Tom also got involved in some charity work. He recorded 'All You Need Is Love' for the charity Childline in 1993, with Kiki Dee, no less, contributing backing vocals. In addition to this, he also recorded a version of the Rolling Stones's 'Gimme Shelter' with the New Model Army to raise money for a homeless project. In many ways, the charity work was a good move, not least because for all his talent, he had also been exceptionally fortunate and he knew it. It was a way of giving something back

As interest in him continued, so people remained fascinated by his rather unconventional marriage. Had he, he was asked in an interview, ever been in love with one of his numerous con-

158

quests? 'Oh no, no, no,' said Tom hastily, for he is not a foolish man. 'I can't say that. You see, my wife doesn't want to know. My wife has never been unfaithful to me, and I don't ask any questions that I don't want to know the answers to. And she doesn't ask me. It's fair that way. She doesn't want to see pictures of me in the papers. Of course I've been attracted to other women. "Don't you go running off with some girl," she says. It's the young thing that bothers her – all women worry about that. Men age gracefully.'

Tom's attitude towards women could be a little odd. It was not just his womanising; he seemed to struggle with seeing women on equal terms. He said it was out of respect for them, but even so, it had the ring of the lad from the Welsh valleys about it. 'I can't even argue with a woman,' he said. 'It makes me hot under the collar. I get emotional and physical. If a woman disagrees with me, I have to ask her, "Who do you belong to?" and address her husband or boyfriend. You argue with the man, you fight with him, you tell her to shut up.'

But the one and only woman this didn't seem to apply to was Linda. 'When I'm with Linda,' said Tom, 'I give her my time. And I take the flak. She gives me flak. I don't think any man in his right mind, unless he's a bully, could think he's got the upper hand with his wife.' This was almost certainly true. For all that Linda has so often been portrayed as the little woman at home waiting for her boisterous husband to reappear, the truth is that she was more than capable of giving as much as she got. Indeed, this was made graphically clear in an interview given by Tom in 2006. Far from being the docile doormat who simply accepted her husband's affairs, Linda became as angry and upset as any woman would have in the circumstances, at one point actually turning on him violently, which is probably what he deserved. He admitted as much himself. 'She beat me up physically one night,' he said. 'I said, "Look, I'm sorry," and she'd got the newspaper there. She said, "You..." I said, "There it is [pointing at chin]," and she went "Bang!" And then she started kicking me.' Rather wisely under the circumstances, he decided not to fight back. 'I took it,' he said.

Tom was not an emotional man, in public, at least, but he was keen to emphasis that he could be as hurt by life as anyone else and he was capable of great distress and crying over those he had loved. 'No, no, no, no, no,' he said, when asked if he tried to avoid emotional engagement. 'I've been upset and faced it – when my father died, when my manager Gordon Mills died. He discovered me; he was like a blood brother. He wrote, "It's Not Unusual" and it nearly choked me to perform it for months after. I also cried when my dog died. It was a black Labrador and it got run over in 1978. I've always had dogs. I like a dog, a Labrador or Alsatian, but I've never had one since, it upset me too much.' It was telling, though, that no crying over women was mentioned here. Tom remained a man's man, through and through.

He was also as upfront as ever about the way he performed on stage. 'My act is the closest thing to sex that I do,' he said. 'The adoration from the fans is very sexual. My ego needs it; I thrive on it. My biggest fear is that someone will stop me. I have dreams where I am locked up, I murder someone; I hide the body, anything to stop me being locked up. After my stage show I just dive in the shower and feel like I've performed some great sexual act. I don't think I would have got where I am today without being so attractive to women.' Comment is perhaps superfluous.

And he was looking pretty good on it all, considering how frenetic his life had been. He has made no secret of the fact that the surgeon's knife has helped him maintain his extremely good looks. Indeed not only was the middle-aged Tom better looking than the young one, but he didn't even much resemble the young Tom; he also kept himself healthy, too. There were the constant workouts, the care he took of his voice – humidifiers accompanied him everywhere to make sure the air was never too dry – and although he liked a drink as much as ever, he never let it go too far. He had never touched drugs, and was faintly appalled by the suggestion he might. 'I was in the toilet and this guy pushed something into my pocket,' he related. 'I didn't know what was going on. I looked in and found folded money and cocaine. I tell you, I just began to shake. I thought it was a bloody set-up.'

On another occasion, he revealed he had never had the desire to use drugs, either. 'They never interested me,' he said. 'I just stick to the booze. Me and the band will be sitting in the lobby of a hotel, drinking the sun up, lifting our feet up on to the tables so they can do their dawn Hoovering underneath us. In fact, whenever we hear the hum of Hoovers in the background, I always say, "They're playing our song, lads. Time for bed.'"

Even so, it was a regime that would have done for many a younger man. Tom was proving lucky here, too: he simply came across as being much younger than he actually was, with the energy of a man half his age. His obvious enjoyment of what he does helped, too. He maintained his fitness not only through his exercise regime, but also because of the sheer amount of energy that went into putting on his act. That energy fed into the audience before being transmitted back to him. It was a phenomenal way for a man in his fifties to behave and perform. But not only was he showing no signs of letting up, his career was becoming more successful than ever before. How long would he be able to continue? For as long as he could sing and stand, in all likelihood. Tom has spent his life doing what he loves most and what he is best at – singing and performing. And the best was yet to come.

CHAPTER 10

TOM ROCKS

As the nineties progressed, Tom's career went from strength to strength under Mark's highly capable guidance. It is safe to say that he was now more popular than he had ever been. His voice still thrilled and his sex appeal remained un-diminished. Needless to say, the latter was still getting him into trouble. The latest to submit to the strength of the Jones's charm was Nicole Hall, a mere thirty-three years his junior, with whom he was pictured at various American hotels. Hall was twenty, but had met Tom when she was just fifteen, and was clearly smitten. 'I live for the times I'm with Tom, he's so much fun,' she is said to have told a friend.

Nicole worked in a health club, and according to friends this particular liaison had been going on for some years. 'They've been an item for a couple of years and see each other regularly. For obvious reasons they don't advertise their relationship and have so far managed to keep it a secret. When Nicole was fifteen, her grandmother took her to Las Vegas and introduced her to Tom. They dated for the first time two years ago and since then they've been together two or three times a year.'

There followed various lurid eyewitness accounts about who stayed in what hotel when, along with sightings of passionate farewells. To seasoned Jones's watchers, it was par for the course, but when she was confronted with revela-tions about the trysts, Nicole initially came over as exceedingly coy. 'Tom is not my lover, he is like a father to me,' she said. 'I have known him since I was fifteen and we're just very good friends. We were introduced by my grandmother, a great fan, who took me to several of his concerts. Why shouldn't we go jogging together? After all, I do work in a health club. Fitness is my business. I'm not denying I went to some of Tom's concerts and spent some time with him. But there is nothing more to it than that.'

It was put to Nicole that the two had checked into at least three hotels together, something that caused an irritated outburst in return. 'That's none of anybody's business,' she said. 'What goes on in my life or his life is nobody's business but ours. I've known him for a long time. He's been a friend of my grandmother's for twenty years and that's the nature of our relationship. I don't explain my actions to my parents, I don't explain my actions to my friends, nor will I explain my actions to a paper thank you very much.' And with that the phone was slammed down.

Dorothy Woodward, for one, was unmoved by the news and the effect it would have on Tom's relationship with Linda. 'I can't see them ever splitting up,' she said. 'They are as happy as any-one else. Linda has come to terms with putting up with his way of life. That's certainly not going to change after thirty-seven years of marriage.' And Tom himself was as keen as ever to stress that the marriage was going to last. 'I'd be lying to say my head wouldn't be turned if some young great-looking bird said she wanted to be with me,' he announced. 'But I would have to say, "I'm sorry, if you're talking about marriage, forget it 'cause I'm in love with my wife." That's a fact.'

He was well aware of the impact he had on his fans, too. 'The thing is, that for most of my fans, the Tom Jones that they go and see is a fantasy, you know? It's something that they look forward to and enjoy while it's happening. But if I ever jumped off-stage while someone was screaming,

"Get your kit off!" and got my kit off and suggested, um, naughty things, they'd run a mile. They don't actually want me, they just want to think about doing it with me.' Modest he wasn't, but he was probably right.

And still he managed to keep his feet on the ground. He had a very self-deprecating streak of humour, and so it was that in 1992 he allowed himself to be kidnapped by Mr Burns in an episode of *The Simpsons*. By now he was enormously rich – his fortune estimated to be about £150 million but still he returned to Wales, and went out with his old friends for a drink in the pub. There were no airs and graces here, and the boys looked after him, too. 'The fellows I went to school with get very protective,' said Tom. 'If I go out and have a drink with two or three of them and somebody comes over and starts bothering me, it's, "Just a second, the man's here to have a drink – leave him alone!" Which is fine.'

It said something for his character that the men would behave like that in the first place. Britain is notoriously unpleasant to her favoured sons and daughters. The ones who make it – especially on the same scale as Tom – are often treated quite badly. Jealousy is prevalent in British circles, even in Wales, and in the early days he encountered some aggression as his star began to shine. But despite the difference in the way he and his old friends lived, he managed to retain the friendship of the men who had known him when he was a nobody and that was something of which he could justly be proud.

His relationship with Linda, which continued to

165

mystify so many, was also a case of keeping his feet on the ground, as he explained. 'A lot of fellows get led astray,' he said. 'Big stars don't want to take any stick from anybody. They have everyone telling them they're great, and if anyone says they're not great, they'll elbow them. The one who's going to bring you down to earth is your missus. She's going to say, "You're with me, now, forget about all that nonsense." My wife loves my talent. But I'm Tommy Woodward when I walk in the room.'

As for the other women – well, matters carried on as they always had done. 'People say, "How the hell do you and your wife stay together?" he said. 'I just say, "Well, that's the way it is. I don't want to walk away from her and she doesn't want to walk away from me. We're together because we want to be. It's as simple as that. My wife won't read the tabloids. She just doesn't want to know. She says, "It's all stupid. As long as you're here, that's what matters."'

Tom was extraordinarily good-humoured about the way people wrote and spoke to him, too. He never got annoyed, never got upset, and on the whole he fielded the questions as gracefully as could be expected and was charm personified, even when feeling grouchy or tired. Anyone less secure in their own skin could have been riled at some comments directed at him but he would give back as good as he got. 'Will you get annoyed if I keep going on about women throwing their pants at you?' asked one interviewer. Tom took it all in his stride. 'Well, you know, that happened and while it's brilliant to inspire that kind of reaction, and a marvellous thing to have in your history, it doesn't happen any more,' he said. 'They throw flowers instead, which is more dangerous, because if you slip on one of those, you execute a disgraceful slide across the stage and end up in the wings.'

Did it annoy him, he was asked, that people turned up to see Tom Jones the Act rather than Tom Jones the Singer? 'Oh yeah,' said Tom, good-humouredly. 'I mean, I work my balls off on stage, it's a gruelling show, I really push myself, and then you get big cheers for taking your jacket off. It can get annoying.' So why not keep it on? 'I sweat,' he replied, happily. 'I sweat like you wouldn't believe. If I didn't take my jacket off, I'd drown. But it can be fun, just teasing the audience. They'll be screaming, "Get your kit off!" and if it's during a ballad – say, "The Green, Green Grass of Home" – I'll ignore them. But if I'm really going for it, I might twitch the lapels a bit. I'll be thinking, wait for it, ladies, wait for it. And they wait. And at the right moment the jacket comes off.'

Who could not have warmed to that? Therein lies yet another secret of Tom's longevity and success: he refuses to take himself too seriously. He was also happy to admit he could be as star struck as anyone else. Asked if he had ever been nervous about meeting anyone, he replied, 'Oh yeah. I'd been an Elvis fan for so long – I mean, he was The King. I went to meet him in Graceland and I was so nervous.

'I was thinking, he meets all these people who tell him he's the best and how much he means to them; how can I pick the right words so that he knows I mean it when I say that his records changed my life? I was shaking just a little bit as he

167

walked towards me. And as he got nearer, I could hear he was singing my hit record of the time under his breath. And he told me how much he loved my voice.' Not a man given to declarations of emotion, this was very nearly an avowal of love from Tom.

It was extraordinary the way his career just kept going from strength to strength. This new incarnation, in which he mixed old hits with new, was a staggering success. He hosted a television show, *The Right Time* in 1992. Then he signed to Interscope and released *The Lead and How to Swing It,* an album in which he collaborated with, among others, Teddy Riley, Flood and Youth. In 1995 he headlined Glastonbury, while in 1996 he starred in a Christmas special, *Tom Jones – For One Night Only,* which attracted such guests as Toni Braxton, Mark Knopfler and Bryn Terfel, another Welshman with an exceptional voice.

An enormous amount of this was down to Mark, his manager. 'Mark understands my love of music,' said Tom. 'That's the first thing. People have always gone on about the swivelling hips and the sex thing, and I say, "Yes, but what about the sound I'm making?"'

He was not just singing, but appearing on the silver screen, too: He appeared in a number of films: *Mars Attacks!* (1996), *Jerky Boys* (1995) and *Agnes Browne* (1999). Looking back, it's surprising he didn't venture into films more often when he was younger. After all, his great friend Elvis starred in one vehicle after another. It is easy to see him as a leading man: his looks and presence are almost as striking as his voice. But then again, he was so busy that perhaps he simply didn't have the time. Crucially for the success he enjoyed, he remained open to new experiences and ideas. In 1994 he released a new album, *The Lead and How to Swing It*, produced by Trevor Horn, who had previously worked with Frankie Goes to Hollywood and Seal. Flood, who had formerly worked with U2 and Nine Inch Nails, also worked on the album, as did Teddy Riley, who listed among his own stable Bobby Brown and Michael Jackson. It was an impressive line-up and the album was very well received, in particular the song 'If I Only Knew'. Touchingly, he dedicated it to his grandchildren.

These days Tom kept pretty starry company, too. In 1995 he sang for Bruce Willis on the latter's fortieth birthday and the birthday boy himself joined him on stage. A year later they were re-united when Bruce and his then wife Demi Moore went to see Tom play in Wembley. 'Bruce is good,' said Tom. 'He's just like one of the lads. He hasn't got a great vocal range, but he's got a lot of atti-tude and he knows a hell of a lot about Rhythm and Blues music. Last night the Duchess of York was there and Bruce was in the audience, singing. So Fergie said, "Wouldn't you like to get up there with Tom?" And Bruce said, "Listen, that's like a housepainter saying to a Rembrandt, can I just fill in the corner here? I did sing with him once. But that was only because I owned the nightclub."' It was vintage Tom.

Another reason for his continued success was, of course, the fact that he still adored performing, getting up on stage, doing the shows, the acts. He had never taken it for granted, never forgotten that the key to it all was to give the audience a night they would always remember. 'When you start singing a hit song, people recognise it and you get instant applause,' he said. 'So you get into it and you're taken over by the whole experience. I love it. It's something I can't get anywhere else.' It showed, too. And then came yet another success, this one harking back to his earliest days, when he sang the title tracks for films, including *Thunderball* and *What's New Pussycat?* It wasn't quite a cover track, but it was quite possibly the most important song in a film that was to become a smash hit. Released in 1997, *The Full Monty* was originally expected to be just a small-scale offering from the vaults of British cinema. Instead, it became an international success. Tom had his way with probably the most important scene in the film – 'You Can Leave Your Hat On' – the track the men danced to in the final scene when they did, after all, reveal the full Monty. Such was the acclaim that both film and song received that it was released as a single in its own right and became a big hit.

Tom was now so cool he had practically gone through the whole realm of coolness and come out the other side. It was impossible not to be charmed by him. Now he was every bit as popular, if not more so, as the men who worked beside him in the music industry and who were forty years his junior and he was loving every minute of it. One of the most appealing elements to his personality was the fact that he so obviously enjoyed his success and as he moved from one career peak to another, his enjoyment was there for all to see.

Proof, if any more were needed, as to the full extent of Tom's coolness came in 1998, with another single – but this one was not his own. Rather, it was entitled 'The Ballad of Tom Jones' and it was released by the Liverpool band Space, with Cerys Matthews singing the lead. Again, in a moment that harked back to Tom's earliest days, the song was written by one Tommy Scott – not the original, of course, but the front man for The Senators. It was a reminder of the days when he was starting out and quite how far he had come since then.

As he approached sixty, Tom seemed to mellow slightly, a development that continues to this day. After all he really did not have anything left to prove. He had also become that most British of individuals: a national treasure. Any foibles – and, apart from the women, there weren't many – were forgiven. His presence was cause for excitement, for celebration, for feeling that something was about to start. Public affection for Tom was massive: Wales adored its successful son, while Britain as a whole was proud that he was still out there, showing he could teach the younger generation a thing or two when it came to managing a crowd. While undiminished, he now treated his sex appeal with a certain degree of humour. One photo of a performance shows him pulling up his sweater to reveal that famously hairy chest. Women loved it, while their men folk were not unduly perturbed.

Any major differences with Linda had clearly blown over, too. Those divorce rumours, even if they were true, had clearly come to nothing. She was back in LA again, shunning the limelight as much as always, but clearly as attached to her husband as she had ever been – as, indeed, he was to her. The childhood sweethearts from Wales were approaching old age now, and a very rich old age at that, and were seemingly settled and content. Not that Tom had any intention of approaching old age by giving up his music – he enjoyed his career far too much for that. And so, with an eye out for new projects, he decided to start performing with the relative youngsters in the music industry. Not for the first time Tom, a veteran from the sixties, was able to show the younger generation how it was really done.

CHAPTER 11

TOM AND FRIENDS

As always, Tom was willing to try something new. And so it was that his next project, 1999's *Reload*, an album of duets came about. It went down a treat: Tom performed with some of the leading singers of the day and more than held his own.

'When I did "Kiss" with The Art of Noise, it was so successful that I started doing duets on television then with people such as Robbie Williams when we did the Brit Awards last year [1998],' he said. 'Every time I did it, it was successful and people would come up to me and say, we saw you singing with so and so, who are you going to be singing with next? So, the most natural thing was, like, let's do an album like that, because I had never done an album of duets before. This is the first one – *Reload*. We found out who was available, and who wanted to. I wanted the three Welsh bands, you know, Stereophonics, Manic Street Preachers and Catatonia. So I was pleased when they said that they would like to do it.

'Van Morrison I've known for years and worked with before, and he agreed to do it. Robbie, of course, because we had worked together before. And then a lot of people who I'd seen on television, like The Cardigans and Natalie Imbruglia, and people like that. And, let me see, Divine Comedy, Barenaked Ladies, The Pretenders – you know, all those people who I had seen on television. So I picked them out to work with, and as I said, The Cardigans, that was the first single that came off.'

Behind the scenes Tom was also working hard to keep in shape. Now fifty-nine, his diet was as strict as ever, as was his exercise regime. 'I have a gym in my house in LA and I work out using a cross trainer as you burn more calories on that than anything,' said Tom. 'But I don't have a personal trainer.' If he wanted to stay on top, it had to be done. 'Well, what's the alternative?' he asked. 'I'd rather get old than die. The thing I really don't like about it [ageing] is that it will stop me from doing what I do. There's going to come a time when I won't be able to sing as well as I do now. Physically, I won't be able to be as free, as aggressive and passionate, on stage. It hasn't got in my way yet, but there will be a time when I'm feeling aches

173

and pains. And I hope I'll look back and savour what I've done. I hope I'm strong enough and bright enough to accept it if my voice isn't sounding as good. Why go on stage and be half as good as you were?'

Why indeed? But while he hadn't got to a stage where there was any decline in his performance or voice, Tom was at an age when many people start to confront mortality. He had been in the business for decades and was one of the most spectacular success stories of his time, but old age comes to most of us and it was clearly occupying his thoughts. And so many of his contemporaries had gone, too. Elvis had died years previously and in 1998 Frank Sinatra passed away, the last of the Rat Pack to do so. There were few people now who were linked to that era in music history, and Tom was one of them.

'I think about it now, especially when people die,' he said. 'Sinatra's dead now, Elvis is dead, Sammy Davis Junior is dead, Dean Martin ... I knew all these people. I was lucky enough to know Sinatra. At the time you're there, it's exciting. You're meeting these people, you don't think about what it means. But when you get a bit older and they die and you look back, you think, good God, think about the people I met!' And, indeed, the same thing was happening to him with a generation of younger stars. 'They feel excitement to be able to sing with me,' said Tom, rather wistfully. 'To sit in the same room. That's what they tell me. Robbie Williams, he's twenty-four, twenty-five years old. He told me that his mother has all my records. He quotes them back to me.'

Age was having another effect, too. While Tom had not, by any means, lost interest in women, he was not quite as active as he had once been. 'There are certain things that are good about ageing,' was how he put it. 'It doesn't seem to be as important as it used to be. You come to terms with that. You don't feel like it. You don't feel as horny. In certain ways, getting older is a relief. There's always an upside to everything.'

Another aspect of the ageing process was brought home to him forcibly by his mother. By 1999 Freda, now eighty-five, was in very ill health, something both her children had to cope with. Tom found it hard being away, but it was part of the job: he prayed, he said, that he would be there when she breathed her last. 'But the odds are against it because I travel so much,' he said. 'She is so proud of me still and – though her mind wanders a bit – she knows us all. Her doctors say that is all we can hope for now. She has told us she wants to be buried in Wales, and I shall get my father out of the ground in Los Angeles and take him back with her. That is what she wants and that is what she will get.'

This was very much Tom as a family man. Ever since he had begun to earn serious money, he had always looked after his parents and sister, and he was more determined than ever to act as the good son. His money made it possible, but that was not the point. There is a side to him that is very traditional and old fashioned. Not only would he want to look after his family because it was the natural thing to do, but also because it was the right thing to do. And, having seen the hardship in which his parents were brought up, he seemed determined to make up for it in any way he could. Tom was a good son, and a good brother. He had not let his family down.

The issue of ageing also came up *vis-à-vis* Linda. While Tom has worn extremely well, not least because of the huge amount of effort he puts into preserving his appearance, Linda has not taken the same approach. Perhaps she feels there is no point: when she was young and pretty her charms did not stop Tom from philandering and now, as a recluse, she is very rarely glimpsed in public. 'She is a pretty woman, still,' said Tom. 'But I think women dread being older and it doesn't sit well with her.' Could she not have surgery? 'Yes, but she won't do that, you see,' said Tom, himself no stranger to the surgeon's knife. 'She has to do things in her own way. I can't tell her. She said to me recently, "Maybe you need a younger person to travel with." She meant that if I wanted a younger wife, she would have to deal with it. I don't need to show off with a young woman like some men do. Whatever flings I've had have never been planned. As long as I reassure my wife that I am married to her and that nothing will alter that, everything is fine.'

Age brings its own fears, though, and even Tom wasn't exempt from that. He had a cancer scare, which actually just turned out to be an old appendix scar – but still. It was a reminder that he, too, was mortal. 'I had been worried about it,' said Tom. 'I was shopping when they rang me with the result. They said all was fine and I thought, thank f*** for that! So me and a guy who works for me went to the nearest bar. When we got back, we were in my garage at home and we were playing some new tracks of mine really loud.

'There's a big fridge in the garage stuffed full of British beer. I was pissed by then. All of a sudden, I hear this little voice going, "Tom, Tom!" I look out of the gate and there's this little face peering over the top saying, "It's Robbie." I explained to him I was sorry but I was drunk because I'd had some good news and that I wouldn't normally be that pissed at that time of the evening. I think he wondered what the hell was going on. I told him to come and look at my bar because there was a picture of me and him at the Brit Awards up there. I've got me and Frank, and me and Elvis up there but the one of him hadn't been put up yet, because a guy was getting it framed. I was saying, "Where is it, where is it?" and I bet he thought I was bullshitting. But even though she's met him before, my wife wouldn't see him. She locked herself in the bedroom. She's a nervous person, even in her own house.'

As he got older, Tom was also looking back more, reflecting on what had made him the man he was. Both his parents had loved singing, although in different ways: his father had a strong voice, while his mother was a natural born entertainer. It was hardly surprising that he turned out in the way he did. 'I got the combination,' he said. 'When my mother got up to sing, she would incorporate some movements. I remember her singing "Silver Dollar" – she'd give it all that business. My father had a better voice than my mother, but he was inhibited. When we asked my dad to sing, he'd say, "Oh, all right, in a minute." My Uncle George, his brother, had more of a way with a lyric: he would sing a song better. My father would sing sitting down, but my Uncle George, he'd have to get up. I was taking notice of all of that.'

Tom was also certain that it was his marriage that gave him the courage to make something of himself, ironic as that might seem to some eyes. The second Linda knew she was pregnant, Tom knew he was going to marry her, but he didn't have a problem with that. He was resolute that matrimony had made a man of him. 'I wasn't bothered,' he said, on finding out about the pregnancy. 'Her being pregnant and us being married made me more determined, I think. All of a sudden, it's like I was a man. Looking back, I desperately wanted to be a man from when I was a kid. There were these older fellows that I was a bit frightened of, who'd say, "Piss off, you're only kids," and I'd think, ooh, one of these days I'll show them. I remember going to the hospital and seeing Linda with my baby and it was like, nobody can touch me now. I'm a man. It gave me more drive, more determination. I had my own family; there was a bigger need in me now to succeed. I had to take care of my wife and child. I don't know if I'd stayed single whether I would have pushed on. Maybe.'

And that is another reason why Tom has never left Linda: their marriage has made him what he is today. As he got older, he has become increasingly prone to bouts of introspection and aware that he has had an extraordinary life and career. The great shame of it is that while his marriage clearly worked so well for him, Linda does not seem to enjoy the trappings of wealth and success that he has brought her way. The fact is that for all the riches open to her, she would almost certainly rather that Tom had stayed plain Tommy Woodward, living with his family in Wales. She had no idea she was marrying a future global superstar and it is hard to escape the conclusion that sometimes she has found it all a bit much.

In his own way, Tom seems to understand. While he might spend most of his life on the road, as he himself has remarked on numerous occasions, when he is with Linda, he really is with her. Their time together is her time, which frequently means taking part in domestic duties which one would hardly associate with the flamboyant T Jones. Shopping is one such activity that the two do together. 'I say to her, "Why doesn't cook take you out? Why don't you get this stuff done when I'm not here?"' he said. 'If I'm having a few days off, time to me is precious. But if she's choosing curtain fabric, she wants me to be there. It's nothing I can't handle. It's just those things that are tedious to me, but important to her. So I do it when I'm there.'

Not that he was there very much. Despite brooding about it, age was not withering him, and he was on the road as much as ever. He was also becoming increasingly outspoken about drug use, not least because, associating with a much younger crowd professionally, he must have seen it more and more. Not only this, he also knew what it could do to people, and his own career longevity might well never have happened if he himself had succumbed. 'It's the body language, see,' he explained. 'It's not attractive. I don't like the smell of marijuana and I don't like the way people smoke it. I don't like the look of someone sniffing cocaine: it looks like a miser thing. I like standing at bars – as opposed to sitting down – smoking a cigar and drinking a cognac.'

Indeed, the surprisingly domestic side to him spread well beyond his periods at home with Linda. Even out on the road he had his fastidious side. 'I'm a pretty neat person,' he confessed. 'I don't like things out of order. I've got to fold towels in the bathroom, pull the bedspread up after I get out of bed – I don't like it hanging on the floor – and puff the pillows up. My upbringing, I suppose.'

Indeed, it was a clear sign that Tom's Welsh background played as important a role in his life as it ever had done. On another occasion he remarked, 'I don't want the maids coming in and thinking, Tom Jones is a slob. So I make the bed, fluff the pillows up, fold the towels... I like the staff to think that I am a tidy chap, so the room has to look as nice as I can make it.'

Professionally, age was far from taking its toll. Tom's new career as a duettist continued to flourish, as when he worked with Cerys Matthews in a highly successful partnership for *Reload*, something he analysed when the scale of its success became apparent. 'Well, Cerys picked it, you know,' he said of their song together, 'Baby It's Cold Outside'. 'I played her about three or four songs, and that was the one she picked. And I'm glad she did, because it worked very well for the both of us. We sang it first on a Jools Holland show on television just to see if it would work or not, and it did, and got a big reaction, and so we then recorded it. We recorded it twice. We tried to do a modern version of it, but it didn't work.

'We both agreed that it had to be done the way it was written. You know, with a big band, and do it all at the same time. It was almost like stepping back in time, because the band was there at the same time we were, which is very rare nowadays. But we all played, you know the band played and we sang. And we came out with what we've got, which I'm very pleased about, I should say. And the video is great as well. I mean, it's a different kind of video. So it's great, and Cerys is a great girl.'

It was all good stuff. Tom was thoroughly enjoying his new collaborations: the novelty of what he was doing was keeping him as energised as ever. Not that he didn't, from time to time, return to the past. Another very successful collaborator was James Dean Bradfield, with whom Tom returned to his former styles. 'I don't think there is anything more powerful on there *[Reload],*' he said. 'We took it up into a high key because it is higher than the way Elvis did it. James said that he would like to do an Elvis Presley song and I said great, because I know all Elvis Presley's stuff. And then when he said "You're Right, I'm Left, She's Gone", I thought, well it's like a rockabilly thing. And then I thought, well, fine, maybe he wants to play that kind of guitar, you know. But then when I got in the studio and he played me the track that he had laid down, I could see that he was pulling

181

it into a heavier rock mode.

'And I said, "Why take it that high?" He said, "Because it will be more dramatic." And I said, "Well it's high, though." And he said, "Yes, well 'Delilah' is high." I said, "I know, but that was thirty-odd years ago!" Because he sings high, James Dean Bradfield. So he said, "You can sing that high," and when I sang it, I realised I could because it is high. But it is more dramatic, and then that creates ... it is perfect, I think.'

In 1999 Tom was given the first of a number of well-deserved honours: he was granted an OBE. This was, however, rather overshadowed by yet another marital indiscretion – he had had a fling with a lapdancer, Christina, who later kissed and told. 'It was encore after encore,' she announced, flattering for a sixty-year-old grandfather, but a little bit embarrassing as well. 'Well, of course, I don't like all that, especially now I have grand-children,' said a slightly embarrassed Tom. 'It's not nice for them to be told their granddad is in the paper with some woman. I tell myself it will never happen again, but sometimes it does. I don't go out to do it. I'm not aiming for it. It's a spur of the moment thing, when I'm not thinking straight. I have to be on my guard, and the older I get, the more on my guard I am.'

Linda, alas, was not with her husband when he received his OBE. For decades now, she had been reclusive, but somehow it seemed almost to have got worse in recent years. Tom never seemed to see this as a problem, either for him or for her, but he conceded that perhaps, had they had a bigger family, or if Linda had had a daughter, life might have been easier for her. But it was not to be.

In his own way, he did try to make life as easy for Linda as he could. She was becoming increasingly lonely as she grew older, not least because her father-in-law was dead, her mother-in-law ailing and her son, who had his own family, was out on the road with her husband. Tom did what he could to help. 'In the end she was stuck in a big old house, with only the people who worked there,' he said. 'She spends her time fixing it up. Not having to worry about money has been a big thing for her. If she wants clothes or something for the house, she can go to Saks and get it.

'But not by herself – she wants me to be there. I'm on the road so much I feel that when I'm home, it's her time. Whatever she wants, I'll do. I coax her sometimes to go to a function, but she says no. She can't be in a room full of people she doesn't know. She'll be fine if we bump into someone like Jack Nicholson at a restaurant, but if she knew he was going to be there, she wouldn't go. I understand what she goes through. She is a shy person and it's been difficult for her to deal with me socially. She can't be part of what I do.'

It was suggested to Tom at one point that rather than being simply shy, Linda might actually have some kind of psychological condition that could be treated. Certainly, her behaviour did sometimes seem a little extreme. Once, when Tom was due to spend a month in London, he bought her a first-class air ticket to come and see him and the family, including the two grandchildren. As ever, Linda couldn't bear to go, although she left it to just three hours before the flight to announce her decision.

'She couldn't come later, because she can't travel on her own,' said Tom. 'There are people who would put her on the plane and meet her from it, but she has a fear of being alone with strange people on an airplane.' Could this actually be neurosis? 'Oh, sure,' said Tom. 'Only I don't look at it that way because I know what she goes through. She is too scared to do these things. I've told her if she's frightened of certain things, she should talk to someone who would get her over it. But she won't do it.'

Tom clearly loves Linda and clearly believes he really does as much for her as he can, but she is also his one blind spot. Had he been a more faithful husband, it is entirely possible that she would not have felt the need to retreat from the world – after all, in the early days, she was perfectly happy to be photographed and interviewed alongside the young performer. But the growing realisation that her husband was never going to be faithful and, at times, not even that discreet about his affairs either, must have had the effect of grinding her down over the years. Tom is not a cruel man and probably the last person he would ever want to hurt is Linda. But it is she, not her husband, who has had to make a massive sacrifice for his fame.

CHAPTER 12

THE REWARDS OF A
LIFE WELL SPENT

As Tom's personal fortune grew, he maintained a surprisingly down-to-earth attitude towards his wealth. 'I don't know what I'm worth, but it's a lot,' he said. 'The great thing about making all that money is that it gets out of the way. You don't have to worry. If you want a diamond ring, you can go and buy it. But you get past that once you have jewellery boxes full of the stuff. How many watches can you wear? Same with cars and houses. It's just a headache to have more than one home.'

In 2002, Tom had another album out, *Mr Jones*, this one done in collaboration with Wyclef Jean. 'I am very proud of it, as there is a lot of me in it,' said Tom. 'It was more of a collaboration than I have done before. I always work at one album at a time because I want to find out from the people how this is received. You never know. You do the best you can and you hope people are going to feel it the way I felt it when I recorded it. But it doesn't always work like that, and you get so close to stuff when you are recording it, you can't stand back and listen to it as other people will. Once I get this album established, then I'll think about the next one.'

Tom had a much greater input into the writing

of this album than he had done in the past, something that Wyclef managed to bring out of him, with the result that he was very proud of a track called 'The Letter' in which the world was given a glimpse in to a very different Tom from the one it has known publicly: a more reflective Tom prepared to meditate on how the impact of some of his behaviour might have affected those close to him.

'The song is important to me because of what it says,' said Tom. 'Wyclef asked me to write a letter to a girl, telling her how I felt about her. He told me to put my wife's name in it. I said, "If I put my wife's name in it, it's going to be about her and it's going to be too personal." But I tried it. The song should have been, "Linda – I ain't too proud to apologise for the things that I've done." But I realized that if I used her name, she'd say to me, "What are you talking about? What are the things you've done?" I didn't want to get into that situation, so I used, "Baby" instead of "Linda." But "The Letter" does make me think about my wife.' Whether close to remorse or not, Tom denied he was ashamed of anything he'd done.

Tom was also rather proud of the fact that he and Wyclef had worked on a new version of 'What's New Pussycat?'. 'It is going to be his next single,' he revealed. 'He wanted to use the original recording, so he sampled me singing it and wrote a new song around it, really. It is about all kinds of cats now. It is a fantastic idea.' As for his old hits, Tom still enjoyed listening to them. 'I listen to them from time to time, just to hear what I sounded like, and what they were like,' he said.

186

'Especially now they are on CD with the *Greatest Hits*. It's much easier than digging the old vinyl out.'

There really were signs, however, that he occasionally had the odd moment of regret about the many women in his past. He never said as much – he probably couldn't – but there were moments when he came awfully close to some kind of remorse. 'Normally men are the predators, the chasers,' he said. 'Women want love, men want sex – I know women want sex as well, but they wouldn't go out of their way to get it. That's why there are prostitutes. There are no male prostitutes.

'OK, young, good-looking fellas for old women, maybe, or for homosexual men, but since the beginning of time there have been prostitutes because men want sex so much they will pay for it. When you become a celebrity, the role is reversed all of a sudden and you have these women wanting to be with you. Men are men and if you're a real man, then...' This was a theory Tom had voiced in the past, and there was probably quite a lot to it. But these days, he seemed keen to downplay what had gone on, perhaps in a very belated bid to minimize the hurt.

'But you don't want to broadcast it, not really,' he said. 'You don't really want to hurt anybody, so that's a part of my life I keep to myself. I don't know what Linda thinks – she doesn't say anything. But she wouldn't go along with me having affairs, I know that for a fact. So, it's never really brought up because it doesn't have to be. I'm a human being, I'm a man.'

187

Most women wouldn't go along with it, but there was still some concept of honour and logic in what Tom said. In his eyes, he was playing by the rules, or some version of them, anyway, in which the man got to do what he wanted, but if he was a decent fellow, he would try not to let it have too much impact on his wife. 'I avoid affairs more than anything else, because I don't want to interfere with my marriage,' he said. 'I love my wife and I wouldn't want her to get fed up and not love me any more. If my wife wants to travel with me she can – she used to a lot. She doesn't have a problem with the booze, but she does like a drink, particularly at night in front of the TV She's not crazy about going out because there are people there. She does like the finer things, though, she loves what my success has brought.'

That much was true. Tom might have had extremely traditional views about the role of men and women within a marriage, but Linda entirely agreed with them. Neither had been very happy about the early days, in which she had had to go out to work. 'My wife doesn't want to work and she never did,' said Tom. 'I like it like that. When I first moved to London, I wasn't making enough money to send home to my wife, so she had to go out to work in a factory. She hated it. She didn't like the fact that she had to leave the house, or that my son would come home and she wasn't there. [After 'It's Not Unusual' hit No.1.] It was as if God had said, "There you are. This is it." I was a professional singer and didn't have to worry about my wife working any more.'

It was a way of life that suited both of them

Initially, Linda had been as excited as Tom about his success, not least because, No. 1 single or no, back then it would have been impossible to predict quite what an extraordinary career her husband was to have. Tom had, by now, entered the realms of the super rich, with estimates of his wealth higher than ever, now at about £350 million. Whatever else his fame entailed, he certainly managed to provide for his family. Those early days, in which Linda had to work in a factory, were a lifetime away. This wealth, in particular, also showed in Tom's features. He now had the indefinable aura of the phenomenally rich about him: the glow that comes with knowing you will never have to worry about where the next penny comes from ever again in your life.

By now, he had been in the business for nearly four decades, an extraordinary achievement in such a fickle business. His explanation is simple. 'I am versatile and I like a lot of different kinds of songs,' he said. 'Some bands are in one kind of area and want to stay there. But I've always liked a wide variety of stuff. A lot of people who started in the '60s are still there, but I wanted to move on. I still do a lot of the songs I did then on stage. Trying new things is what keeps me going: it is more exciting and more challenging. But I only try the stuff I think I can do. I wouldn't try to change my style.'

Another reason for Tom's longevity was that, as he said himself, there was no mystery surrounding his public persona. 'With me, I think what you see is what you get,' he said. 'I don't change my image when I walk in the house. There is, of course, more effort when you go on television, or in the recording studio, or when you do live shows. You put your energies into the time allotted to you, but I don't change. My attitude is the same.'

Here, Linda was a factor. She didn't let him forget where he'd originally come from and how he'd started out. 'My wife fell in love with Tommy Woodward and she doesn't let me forget it,' he said. 'A friend of mine came over one evening and we were playing pool. I suppose I was getting a bit drunk and being a bit "Tom Jones," going on about New York. Linda said, "Just a minute, you don't really think you're Tom Jones, do you? I didn't marry Tom Jones, I married Tommy Woodward, so, if I'm sitting here, don't talk like that." Funnily enough, though, the other day we were watching someone relaxing at home on TV and she said, "That guy's letting himself down, allowing himself to be seen like that." I said, "He's only a human being. I'm more relaxed when I'm at home." She replied, "Whatever you do, you're still Tom Jones. You just carry yourself in a different way." I wasn't even aware of it. I thought I was very basic at home. But she still seems to think I'm Tom Jones. To her I have this thing. Maybe that's why she fell in love with me to begin with – because I have this thing.'

But still he was aware of the effects of getting older. He had no wish whatsoever to retire, and so he was enormously careful of voice. 'I go and see my ears, nose and throat doctor just to make sure my voice is OK,' he said. 'I drink lots of water and try to get eight hours sleep every night I avoid

190

things that might hurt it. I'm not a fanatic, but I would hate to lose my voice because it gives me so much pleasure and it's my strength. Sometimes, when I listen to my recordings, I think, "I didn't plan that" and I'm amazed.' From someone else that might have sounded conceited, but Tom, as ever, managed to come out on the right side of charm.

He also was quite open about the fact that he'd had a fair bit of plastic surgery, including teeth capping and a scalp reduction to reduce the signs of incipient balding. 'They just take the part of the scalp where the hair's thin, cut it out and sew your head back together again,' was his cheery explanation. 'Things look better to me at night. I don't like mornings and I tend not to want to go to bed. I think it's a time thing – I don't like thinking about time. I used to party a lot, but now other things are more important than they used to be. When I was younger, food was just a necessity, not a pleasure. If I was hungry, I would eat quickly so I could go to a club. Now, I enjoy a long dinner in a nice restaurant – a Martini to start, fine wine, a Cognac, a Cuban cigar. I'm a night person.'

Tom had always been seen as something of an ambassador for Wales, and these days even more so. His songs were now played before Welsh rugby internationals, which delighted him. 'It makes me feel very proud, especially when it is sport and especially when it is Wales,' he said. 'When I sang when Wales played England, that was my contribution to the match – I think I can sing better than I can play rugby.' Asked if he would consider moving back to Wales from the United States, he replied, 'Yeah, I would think so. But for me, I haven't really left. Having a house in Los Angeles is just where the house is. I have a green card – I still have a British passport. I haven't become American; it is just more convenient for me living there. I carry Wales around with me.' Everything but the language, that is. 'My grandfather spoke Welsh, but in south Wales when I was brought up, it was so cosmopolitan,' said Tom. 'I might learn Welsh anyway now, because I should be able to speak it, and I always feel a bit guilty of the fact when Catherine Zeta Jones talks to me and I can't converse with her in Welsh.'

Indeed, Tom was enormously proud of his Welsh heritage and lost no opportunity to talk about the land of his fathers and its phenomenal musical traditions. 'I always thought that South Wales, there was always a lot of talent there, in the clubs and pubs and where I started singing,' he said. 'So I was always aware of that. Especially vocalists, there have always been strong voices in Wales, it's just that they were not as successful outside of Wales. And that is something that has been straightened out now of late, because of the bands that are coming out of South Wales. And they are writing their own material, which was never done before.'

All this he was watching with some interest. While his had been the traditional rise to fame of the time – an outstanding singer who performed the music others wrote for him – now all that was beginning to change. 'I mean, even when I came out of Wales, I wasn't writing the material, but Gordon Mills was, who was another Welshman,' he said. 'So it was still definitely a Welsh thing. Stereophonics are a great band, straight ahead Rock'n'Roll band, you know, like I was when I was singing in South Wales; when I was singing with The Senators. They're very similar. And they were telling me that, because I used to rehearse in a pub in Abercynon called The Thorn Hotel, and they used the same pub.

'And they said, is it true that you used to rehearse in The Thorn? I said yeah. They said, well that's where we rehearse. It's a strange thing: of all the pubs in South Wales, we happened to pick on the same one. The Stereophonics are a great bunch of boys. It's very natural, they're very straight ahead. And so is the Manic Street Preachers and so is Catatonia, you know. They're very Welsh and proud of it, and there's a lot of fire in what they record and what they perform. So it was great to work with these people.' It is noticeable, incidentally, that Tom was not just talking about his Welsh heritage: he was also showing that he was totally up to date with what was going on musically. It was yet another of the reasons that he had always stayed at the top.

But he was very pleased that so much talent was Welsh. 'Well, I think, as I was saying about Welsh music, it is fantastic now,' he said. 'Stronger now than ever. And I love the people who are doing it. You know, James Dean Bradfield, I think, is a great singer and guitarist, and so is Kelly with the Stereophonics and Cerys is a great singer with Catatonia. So, you know, I'm glad they are doing what they do!'

In 2003, Tom was devastated when his mother

Freda died, aged 88. It had been expected for years, but the loss of a parent is traumatic no matter how old or successful the child and Tom had been particularly close to his mum. At the Brits that year he was due to receive an Outstanding Contribution to Music Award: he decided to use it to make a tribute to his mother, although he was really concerned he might break down.

'He was very upset, but said he was going to carry on with his commitment to go to the Brit awards,' said his cousin Val Davies. 'He said Freda would have wanted him to carry on. Tom's a very emotional person and is devastated at Freda's death – they were very close. I told him if he feels he can't say the words out loud he should just say it to her in his mind. But it would be lovely if he could manage it.' In the event, he did.

As the years went by, Tom's Welsh heritage began to seem even more important to him. 'Wales is considered cool now because of a lot of the talent that's coming out of there, you know,' he said happily. 'I mean, when I first came to London, I think Shirley Bassey was the only one from that part of the world who was recording then. There's always been a lot of talent coming out of there, like Richard Burton, you know, was the biggest actor that came out of there, or star, movie star. You had people like Dylan Thomas, who the Americans were all very aware of because of his poetry.'

Wales, however, was now churning out megastars by the lorry load. Tom once got into trouble when he said he was better acquainted with Malibu than Mumbles, but he was utterly sincere in the delight with which he hailed his fellow Welsh stars. And they like him, inhabited the highest realms of fame: they were international megastars. And they came from Wales. 'Catherine Zeta Jones is the biggest female film star that we have,' said Tom. 'She is huge in America, and you know, she flies the flag, God bless her. She lets everybody know that she is Welsh. I think Wales, as far as show business is concerned, is cooler now than it has ever been. When you come from South Wales, you're always thinking about it and hoping that there's going to be other successful entertainers coming out of there. I don't think it was ever as successful as it is now.'

This patriotic attitude was dinned into him from an early age. Tom's parents were Welsh and proud of it and they made sure he was, too. 'Our family name was Woodward and I used to bring it up a lot,' said Tom in an interview. 'I would say, "Why does nana speak funny?" and my father would say, "She's not from here." "Where's she from?" "England." "Why is that?" I was one of those kids. I said "If your mother's English and your father's English, you're English." He said, "I'm not English, I'm Welsh. I'm a Welsh coalminer, that's what I am."'

Retirement looked as far away as ever. Tom continued to work on new projects, with new collaborators, and was showing a genius for picking the right people with whom to work. Far from making himself appear dated in comparison to these bright young things, Tom was keeping steadily ahead of the pack. It was a brilliant strategy – and a huge amount of credit must go here, too, to son Mark. The next person with whom Tom worked was to prove a perfect foil. It was Jools Holland, with whom Tom recorded a new album in 2004. There were some new numbers and some old Blues and Rock'n'Roll, and Tom was delighted when he played the album to Jerry Lee Lewis, who had been, as it were, their muse.

'He loved it,' said Tom. 'He asked how old Jools was and I said he was in his forties. And Jerry said, "Tell that boy he can play." Coming from Jerry Lee Lewis, that's amazing. He doesn't like other piano players. He thinks he invented boogie-woogie, so I was knocked out by that.' Jools was not displeased with the compliment either. 'Well, I was so flattered,' he said. 'In fact we had to get the builders round, because my head was so big we had to knock a wall out. And one of my hobbies is boasting down the pub, so I was straight down there with something to boast about.'

It was a partnership that worked exceptionally well, and yet it should not have been a surprise. Jools might have been 20 years younger than Tom and a native of England rather than Wales, but their careers had kicked off in markedly similar fashion. They sang the same kind of music, something they discovered when Tom appeared on Jools's *New Year's Eve Hootenanny* TV programme in 1998, and both served their apprenticeship in pubs and clubs as they began to build up a following. And while Jools had never become a global superstar in quite the manner of Tom, he was one of the most respected musicians of his generation with, like Tom, a following that encompassed several different generations. There were the fans of his own age, who knew him right back in the early days, but also a younger crowd as well. Indeed, in these youth-obsessed times, it was noticeable quite how popular the pairing of a forty-something and a sixty-something had been. These are the days of fame without talent, and yet still Tom and Jools managed to knock their fellow singers into a corner.

'This is material that we both loved when we first started doing it,' said Tom. 'I heard a lot of these records when they first came out. It's the kind of stuff that I started doing – Rock'n'Roll, rhythm and blues, soulful ballads.'

It was clear from their initial meeting that here were two men who understood what the other wanted to do. They had very similar tastes, likes and dislikes, and both were prepared to experiment to discover the manner that suited them best. After all, the collaboration was not just a new departure for Tom, but for Jools as well, albeit one that made perfect sense. 'We realised we loved the same songs,' said Jools. 'A couple of years later he came on *Later with Jools Holland* and the same thing happened. Because we found out we knew these songs and they sounded so good, we put them in the show. Then we went to dinner one night and Tom started singing. I could see people straining to see what was going on and I thought, this is mad. We should make a record.'

Of course it took some time for the pairing to take place, not least because both had commitments around the globe, but when it finally did, the results were electric. The two wanted to produce as immediate a sound as possible, to invite the listener to feel he or she is hearing the music in person, rawness and all. 'We wanted to keep it light,' said Tom. 'What we first did in the rehearsal room on Jools's *Hootenanny*, that's what we wanted to record.'

'The other thing,' said Jools, 'is we hope that when you hear this record – because some are old songs and some we've written alongside them – the old songs sound like our reinvention of them. We both really want this album to be recognisably us.' It was, and was recognisably a great success.

Tom's feelings of patriotic fervour were given a further fillip in 2005, when grandson Alex Woodward was selected to represent Wales in the Commonwealth Games as a full bore rifle shooter. The games were to take place in Melbourne, and Alex's involvement, confirmed by the Sports Council for Wales, aroused a good degree of interest, not least because of the young sportsman's famous forebear.

Indeed, Alex had spent his childhood with his parents and grandparents in Los Angeles, before returning to his native shores, but it was in Wales that he first learned to shoot. 'My grandad had a home near Cowbridge [in south Wales] and he had air rifles there,' he said. 'I think I used to shoot little pieces of paper or something. It's quite possible that he was the first person to show me how to use a gun, though both my dad and my uncle did as well. 'I've always been close to my grandad. We're a small family as my dad's the only child and we used to go over to his house all the time when we were all living in LA.'

Would Tom himself be in attendance at the games? Alex was cautious in his reply. 'He's a busy man so I don't know if he could make it halfway round the world,' he said. 'He's never seen me shoot competitively but he loves his sport, especially rugby. He loves going to the games and watching it on television whenever he can. But my entire family are very supportive. My grandfather's very happy that I'm going to the Games. But he's definitely more proud of the fact that it's for Wales than anything else. He just said to me: "Good boy, shooting for Wales."' Indeed, it was quite something for Tom that his status as the world's most famous Welshman was being consolidated by the fact that his son's son was now also a credit to his country.

And so it was fitting that in 2005, Tom returned to Pontyprydd for the first time in forty-one years to sing an open-air gig in Ponty Park, for which he received no fee. It was a highly emotional homecoming, both for Tom and his 25,000-strong audience, who could barely contain themselves when their idol stepped on stage. All the old hits – 'Delilah', 'What's New Pussycat?' *et al* were played, while his audience waved, of course, knickers at Tom, many inscribed with declarations of love.

He was overwhelmed. 'I'm going to be sixty-five in a few days and I can't believe it,' he said. 'I feel like I'm twenty-five again. I'll be an OAP this time next week and here I am singing in front of all of you. The last time I performed in Pontypridd was 30 June 1964, at the White Hart.' To add to the excitement, Welsh opera singer Katherine Jenkins came on stage to present Tom with a giant birthday cake. She then proceeded to sing Happy

Birthday in both English and Welsh. 'Now there's beautiful, and she can sing as well,' said Tom.

It was a homecoming his parents would have been proud of. Tom had not actually been to Wales since his mother had died two years previously, and it was the only concert he was playing in Britain before going on a world tour in which he was scheduled to play 139 different venues. There was something almost symbolic about it: Wales welcoming home her greatest son, with Tom, in reply, avowing his devotion to the land of his fathers. Rarely can there be an event that so combined emotion with good humour. Tom, to all intents and purposes, had come home.

'It must be terribly emotional for him,' said Margaret Sugar, Tom's cousin. 'The fact that he is here singing tonight would have meant the world to Freda. He loved his mother so much.'

Tom himself couldn't have been happier, finishing the show with an encore of 'The Green, Green Grass of Home'. 'It was lovely to see you,' he said. 'God bless you. We have got to do this again.'

As the career of Jones the Voice continued in its own unstoppable way, Tom continued to be courted by a younger generation, all keen to work with him. Next in line was 27-year old Nick Bracegirdle, aka Chicane, with whom Tom recorded his next single, 'Stoned In Love'. 'I wanted him to do something fresh, different, to sing in a way that is newer,' said Chicane. 'It's a huge voice he has got, but he has also got charisma, somehow. Everyone kind of respects him. It's like when he was doing the Brits and Robbie was gushing all over him. He's like the Godfather of Singing and to work with him is pretty special.'

Another of the secrets of his longevity, of course, was that – women aside – he had never indulged in excess. Although his first house in LA had, after all, belonged to Dean Martin, he remembered when it became his own. 'It had two bars and I thought to myself, "Christ!"' he said. 'When I was a kid and saw that in the movies, people drinking at home, I thought that would be something, a bar in your house and crystal glasses, able to have a drink whenever you wanted it. Well, it so happens you can't. Your voice doesn't work if you have drunk too much – mine doesn't, anyway.'

And so Tom, who had always been able to step back from the brink has survived, while Elvis, who hadn't, didn't. Tom reflected a lot about that these days, too. It has been three decades since the King went off to meet his maker and Tom clearly wished he'd been able to help his old friend. Recalling that Elvis once asked him how he coped with his fame, Tom continued, 'I said, "I enjoy it."' Did he take drugs, Elvis wanted to know. 'I said, "I don't. Maybe that's one of the reasons I enjoy it." Elvis said he had tried every-thing, but he didn't say he was still trying it. He wouldn't admit that to me.'

And did Tom ever think he should have done more to save Elvis from himself? 'Only when it was too late,' said Tom rather sadly. 'He was crying out for help, I suppose, but if people tried to tell him he had a problem, he would fire them. Sonny West [a friend of Elvis] came to see me and said, "We're worried about Elvis. We can't get to him. But we're sure you could." I said I would try. But he wouldn't answer my calls. Then he died. You think, maybe, if I had tried a bit harder, pushed a bit more... I saw Red West [Sonny's cousin and another friend of Elvis] a couple of years ago and he said, "We all thought that if anyone could have got to him it would be you. He genuinely liked and respected you."' Although now long ago in the past, clearly the whole episode still made Tom sad, yet there was probably little that he, or anyone else, could have done.

CHAPTER 13

A KNIGHT WITH SIR TOM

'IT'S NOT UNUSUAL TO BE DUBBED BY ANYONE...'

The headlines said it all. Wales's most famous and most popular son had been made a knight of the realm. The transformation from working class hero to pillar of Britain's show business aristocracy was complete. Tom Jones was, at long last, to become Sir Thomas Woodward, recognition – if it were needed – of the depths of Tom's popularity and the public affection in which he is held.

On the big day – 29 March 2006 – Sir T was dubbed on both shoulders with a sword, as is the tradition. His family were there in force, apart, sadly, from Linda, who had not felt able to make the journey. But Tom's sister, son *et al* were on hand, photographed with a beaming Tom, clearly thrilled with the honour he had received. What was also telling was the way that Tom related the experience afterward. His first encounter with the Queen had actually been at the Royal Variety Show in 1966, something HM mentioned as she greeted the newly ennobled Sir Tom. 'It is fantastic; it was lovely to see the Queen again,' said Sir Tom. 'I love seeing the Queen and I have always been a royalist. She is lovely and she is still lovely; she has got a great smile and her whole face lights up when she smiles.' Tom was talking about her with great respect, of course, but the implication was still there: the Welsh miner's son was certainly not intimidated by royalty.

Tom was certainly a massively popular choice for the knighthood. 'I just hoped for it,' said Sir T. 'All you can do is hope; you can never know.' The Queen had asked him how long he had been in show business: 'I told her forty-one years, and she said to me that I had given a lot of people a lot of pleasure. I come from a coalmining, working-class background. My father was a coalminer. Today is just tremendous. When you first come into show business and you get a hit record, it is the start of something. As time goes on, it just gets better. This is the best thing that I have had. It is a wonderful feeling, a heady feeling. Sometimes you just can't believe it, you think you have been dreaming.'

Could a Knight of the Realm really be working class? Tom might have started out that way, but he seemed to have made something of a leap since then. Yet he was still aware of his roots. 'We're working-class people who, through my God-given gift, have money,' he said. 'I believe in God. I used to go to a Presbyterian chapel and my wife was born Roman Catholic. But you don't really have to go to a building to believe in God. God is inside you. I am a Christian.' He continued on his theme. He really had been granted a huge amount in life, and his public avowal of Christianity was an acknowledgement of that. 'If there's one thing I'm proud of, it's my success,' he said. 'God gives you things but you have to do something with them. I'm proud that I did something with my voice and I'm proud that people like the way I sing.'

There was something quite humble and touching in Tom's reflection on his day at the Palace, not least when speaking of his voice as a God-given gift. With no professional training, Tom had become one of the most recognizable voices of a generation, and it was on the strength of this that he now enjoyed his comfortable lifestyle. There was simply no other way he could have escaped the poverty of his background, a fact he was well aware of.

Linda's absence, however, was noticed. This was, after all, the crowning moment in her husband's career, and so it seemed a little unusual for his wife to not be at his side. Tom responded to enquiries of her whereabouts thus: 'I knew Linda wouldn't be at the Palace, because she's scared of flying,' he said. 'After 9/11, she will not fly any more.' The couple were approaching their golden wedding anniversary and it was patently obvious that Linda was the love of Tom's life. She had remained married to the boy she had met when they were

still just children. And however he might have be-
haved in the past, Tom showed a total loyalty to
her emotionally: he had refused to acknowledge
the child he had fathered out of wedlock, but
talked constantly about how proud he is of his son
Mark. Asked about this by one interviewer, he
replied, 'Oh yes, but he's my wife's child.' That,
more than anything else, summed up the bond
between Tom and Linda, still there after all these
years.

The interviewer asked what had kept them
together. It was not, after all, a conventional relationship. 'Love, I suppose,' said Tom. 'And we've
always liked one another. We have a similar sense
of humour because we come from the same place.
I think that has a lot to do with it.'

Nor was Linda quite the downtrodden wife she
may sometimes have been portrayed as being.
Few women could have viewed the behaviour of a
husband like Tom with equanimity, and so it
proved. Tom himself revealed that she'd gone for
him once after reading about an indiscretion: 'She
beat me up physically one night,' he said. 'I said,
"Look, I'm sorry," and she'd got the newspaper
there. She said, "You..." Tom pointed at his chin.
'There it is,' he told Linda. 'And then she went
bang – and then started kicking me.' But while it
might have relieved Linda's feelings, only age was
to change Tom's behaviour. Towards the end of
2006, Tom's next tour kicked off, and it was an
astounding success. It was a measure of his popularity that he was now treated simultaneously as a
sex symbol and national treasure: there was a real
sense of affection emanating from the audience as

he bounded up on stage. Tom was almost appearing as an old friend: he'd been around for so long, done everything, knew everyone and come through it all with such good humour that the sense of goodwill was palpable. The critics loved it, too. 'A commanding stage presence in bespoke blue suit and bright orange face, Pontypridd's answer to Pavarotti did not disappoint,' wrote Stephen Dalton in *The Times*. 'Half bullfighter and half bulldozer, Jones may represent the preposterous pinnacle of ultra-butch heterosexual camp, but he is a million miles away from kitsch. However overblown, camp is always sincere. And Jones the Voice invariably means it.'

Mean it Tom did, but this didn't mean he was immune from experiencing the more bizarre aspects that come with this level of fame. Tom was beginning to rack up the weird and wonderful accolades that attach themselves to long-term members of the show business community. Like his old friend Elvis and John Coltrane, a church in California had been established in Tom's honour, presided over by Pastor 'PJ' Jack Stahl. Pastor Stalh used Tom's music during baptisms, marriages and funerals: 'It's weird, but a positive thing,' said a slightly bemused sounding Tom.

That national treasure status only grew as Tom supported various events in his native Wales, something he appeared to be doing increasingly as time wore on. There was a huge gathering of people with the surname Jones in Cardiff in November 2006, organized by the town of Blaenau Ffestiniog, which had the highest proportion of Joneses in the UK, in which the Welsh capital decided to break a record for gathering the greatest number of people together with the same surname. A record-breaking 1,224 people sharing the surname Jones squashed into the Wales Millennium Centre, breaking the previous record, which had been set in Sweden by 583 Norbergs: Guinness World Record officials were in attendance to validate the attempt. Performers that night included Grace Jones, Dame Gwyneth Jones, Gwyn Hughes Jones and John Owen-Jones; the co-hosts for the night were Blue Peter presenter Gethin Jones and Gwenllian Jones. Tom sent a message (in truth, of course, his surname isn't Jones), to be read to the crowd with messages from other Joneses, such as Bryn Terfel Jones and Aled Jones. Later televised on S4C, the occasion was a massive success.

More than ever, Wales was proud to have Tom as a favoured son: the photographer Terry O'Neill recalled one instance when Tom returned to the land of his birth for a photoshoot. 'It always went down well, that "Tom Jones revisits his Welsh roots" story,' he said. 'In fact, it was so good I think we did it three times altogether. I remember [the first time] we parked that colossal car right across the street outside the house where he'd grown up. We had to do it really early in the morning, because the crowds were clustering round him all the time, and we wanted a clear shot for this one. But there was one old lady who heard the commotion and stuck her head out of her door, wanting to see what was going on. She just wouldn't put her head back in. Those Welsh are so amazingly patriotic.'

In many ways, Wales was becoming more important to Tom than it ever had been. Four decades earlier he'd left to take on the world and win, which he'd certainly achieved. Now he was older, reflecting on his life and what he'd made of it, and the land of his fathers was weighing on his mind. He was making an increasing effort to return in order to mark momentous occasions in his life with fellow Welshmen, to celebrate his life as a boy from Wales.

'I did an open-air concert in Ponty Park for my 65th birthday, which was fantastic,' he remembered. 'I didn't realise how close the hills were to Pontypridd – they seemed bigger and farther away when I was a child. People were up on the hills, the ones that couldn't actually get into the park, and when I did 'The Green Green Grass Of Home' I started tightening up towards the end of the show. I had to try and keep going because the voice tightens up if you get too emotional. I talked about our old house and I pointed to it – I could see it! I love Wales and everybody there seemed very proud. I'm proud to be Welsh too.

'My childhood was a tremendous time for me. I still have a lot of cousins there and the fellas I grew up with, but going in a pub in Pontypridd is not exactly the same because the faces aren't there – not the ones I knew. As a child, I used to sing at birthday parties and with all my cousins getting married, we had all these wonderful weddings. I would get up and sing and the ones that hadn't seen me before would say, "My God! This kid is gonna be a star!" All my other cousins would say, "Oh yeah, yeah, you know, it's only Tom." Only

Tom had done pretty well.

Another reason for Tom's enduring popularity was that even now, with all his money, houses and cars, he kept his feet on the ground. Everyone who met him commented on his unfailing politeness and graciousness, something that had never left him, no matter how well he did. Tom was many things, but he was not a diva, a tantrum-thrower or a spoilt brat. 'I don't like bad behaviour just because you're rich or famous,' he told one interviewer. 'I remember early on I had to get there really early for my TV show and I was moaning away. When I arrived there was this building site, and this kid was going up a ladder carrying a hod, which is what I used to do. And he said, "Hey Tommy, want to give me a hand with this?" I thought, Jesus Christ, I'm moaning, but he's going to be up and down that ladder all day.'

Tom was, however, becoming conscious that he had been a performer for an awfully long time, so the R-word was beginning to rear its head. For a man who had spent so much of his life in the limelight, this was not an appealing prospect. 'I'm not looking forward to retiring,' he asserted. 'The biggest fear for any performer is that it will be taken away from you. It's so much part of you, a physical thing, it's scary to think one day it won't be there any more. If I'm not able to sing, I won't know what to do. There is no alternative to ageing – just death. The only reason I would like to be young is that you've got longer to live. But it's a great feeling to have grandchildren.'

Of course, there was absolutely no need for him

to retire. Tom worked in one of the few professions in which he could set his own retirement age: as long as the audiences flocked to him, and they certainly did that, he could keep going for as long as he wanted. Nor was his energy flagging. When Tom got out there on that stage, he was still the presence he ever had been: there might have been fewer knickers flying towards him, but the adoration that followed him everywhere was as great as ever. The only way Tom would have had to retire was if the public tired of him, and there was no chance at all of that.

Tom appeared to want to be actively involved in the concerns of the local community, especially where Wales was concerned. It was as if, life having given him so much, he wanted to repay something. In early 2007, there was consternation when Burberry announced plans to close a factory in south Wales and switch production to China: Tom, along with other celebrities such as Emma Thompson and Rhys Ifans, stepped in to try to get the company to change its mind. Although still based in LA, he was increasingly bound up in the day-to-day life of his native land and one of a number of big names willing to bring the plight of Welsh workers to the fore, particularly as some of the workforce came from families who had been employed by the company for decades.

The factory was based in Treorchy, Glamorgan: Tom came from Pontypridd, just 10 miles away. 'As a local boy, I know how important this factory has been to the community in the Rhondda,' he said. 'I therefore urge the Burberry management to withdraw their plans to close the Treochy factory.'

Feelings were running high. Burberry executives were called before the House of Commons Welsh Affairs Select Committee, while in the meantime a demonstration was staged outside Burberry London stores in Regent Street and New Bond Street. The Church of England was under pressure to sell its £2.5 million stake in the company, while Tom's contribution to the cause was noted: 'It is great to have Tom Jones backing our campaign, it shows the depth of feeling that Welsh people around the world have for the Burberry factory workers,' said Leighton Andrews, a member of the Rhondda Welsh Assembly.

'Burberry continues to make good profits. They can afford to keep the factory open; they can afford to pay more generous redundancy terms. They can afford to invest in keeping at least some jobs going in a co-operative venture. With the support that is now building up, I can't believe the company will want to face the House of Commons looking like the meanest company in Britain.' Burberry itself was taciturn: 'We are proud of our British heritage and we continue to design and manufacture in the UK,' it said in a statement. It went on to offer to donate the factory to Wales, a move that was welcomed in some quarters and condemned in others as a publicity stunt. But Tom's continuing involvement certainly kept it in the news.

It was quite a while before the matter was resolved. In February 2007, Burberry had been due to hold a reception for Bafta nominees: it was forced to pull out, reiterating that it was a British company and proud to be one. 'We are disappointed because we'd hoped to further support the British film industry and to celebrate on an international stage British creativity in both film and fashion,' said John Peace, Burberry's chairman.

'As a British-based global luxury brand, with a history of actively supporting the British arts, most recently the Hockney exhibition at the National Portrait Gallery, we are very disappointed at the attempts to disrupt this premier event for the British film industry in arguably one of its most successful years. Burberry is wholly committed to Britain, is headquartered in London and its historic, iconic rainwear manufacturing base continues to be in Yorkshire. Almost half of the group's global workforce is based in the UK.'

It was a clear sign that the campaign was having an effect, as Leighton Andrews was only too happy to point out. 'This shows that the campaign is generating deep concern at the highest echelons of Burberry's management,' he said. 'Burberry should take responsibility for their own actions. They are the people disrupting Bafta's plans. It is they who are now withdrawing sponsorship of the event, just as they are the ones transferring jobs from Britain overseas.'

Ultimately the factory did close, but with significant and hard-won concessions: there was an extension of the factory's closure date, enhanced redundancy payments, £500,000 to retrain the workforce and £150,000 to be spent on the community every year for the following decade.

Despite all the wealth and glamour attached to

him, there was a perception that Tom had not forgotten his roots. He still understood the problems of the common man. But he was certainly wealthy. In 2007, he sold a property in Los Angeles that he'd used for visiting friends and family for £2.2 million profit. The four-bedroomed home had a 'black bottomed' swimming pool and parking for ten cars. There were also reports that he and Linda were thinking of returning to the UK, although to date Tom continues to divide his time between Britain and LA. In March 2007, Tom and Linda also celebrated their fiftieth wedding anniversary – it had been quite a ride for them both.

That summer Tom was one of a star-studded line-up to sing at Concert for Diana, the concert put on by Princes William and Harry to mark the tenth anniversary of the death of Princess Diana: he sang a cover of the Arctic Monkeys' 'I Bet You Look Good On The Dancefloor'. Sir Elton John was a fellow performer, along with Lily Allen, P Diddy, Kanye West, Rod Stewart, Take That and Joss Stone. The presenters on the night, which would have been Diana's 46th birthday, were equally starry: David Beckham, Sienna Miller, Kiefer Sutherland and even video tributes from Nelson Mandela and Bill Clinton: it was, with some justification, referred to as the concert of the year.

The night before had been a warm up, of sorts. Elton John held his annual and very starry White Tie and Tiara Ball: Tom was a guest and he and his fellow Welsh superstar Shirley Bassey also provided some of the entertainment – complete with knicker-throwing when Tom went on stage to perform. It was an A-list evening: guests included Elle Macpherson, David Walliams, Frank Lampard, Tracey Emin, Sir Michael Caine and Dame Judi Dench. Guests were given glasses of Laurent Perrier champagne as they strolled through the grounds of Elton's mansion to admire the array of ice sculptures: inside the marquee, where dinner was held, the interior resembled a Las Vegas casino.

In the middle was a massive water fountain: guests at the hundred tables surrounding it dined on asparagus, roast beef, potted shrimps and knickerbocker glories. Stephen Fry compered the night's auction. Items up for grabs included Elton's Rolls-Royce Drophead Coupe (it fetched £800,000), and Audi R8 (£400,000), a tennis lesson with Roger Federer (£325,000) and ten 'Superbrand' boxes with items including Jimmy Choo shoes, Ben De Lisi clothes and a Chopard watch, at £20,000 each.

The most eyecatching item, though, came courtesy of Tracy Emin, the bad girl of British art: she had customised a blanket, which ultimately sold for £800,000: 'I am worth more than a f***ing car, you f***ers!' she bellowed, as the bidding soared ever higher. 'I can't find the stage, where's the f***ing stage?' As the other guests observed, she was standing on it at the time. It was a riotous affair, full of the great and good joking among each other, teasing one another and getting ready for the next day's grand events, in which the eyes of the world would be on the lot of them. Tom was in the middle of it all, contributing to the heady atmosphere and lapping up the admiration of his peers. It was his kind of place, the sort of surroundings in which he shone. He was right at the heart of the show business establishment – and it showed.

CHAPTER 14

TOM TAKES CENTRE STAGE

The party at Sir Elton John's was all fantastic preparation for the concert. Tom trialled his Arctic Monkeys cover in front of the guests: 'I am a massive fan of the band and I felt like doing something different with my set,' he explained. 'It's a great song and I wanted to do it as a surprise for the Princess Diana concert. I haven't been in touch with the lads about it, but I hope they like it.'

They did and so did the rest of the audience, who were clearly determined to have the time of their lives. It was David Beckham who got probably the biggest cheer of the night when he came on to introduce Take That. 'I am truly honoured to be here today to help celebrate the incredible life of the most amazing lady this country has seen for many, many years,' he said. 'She was the nation's lady, the nation's princess, always has been and always will be. I think what the Princes have achieved here is truly remarkable and the nation should be so proud of them.'

It was certainly a lively event. Prince Harry

215

bounded on to the stage at the start of the six hour show: 'Hello, Wembley!' he called to the 63,000 people in the stadium and 500 million in 140 different countries who were watching the proceedings on TV. 'This event is about all that our mother loved in life – her music, her dancing, her charities and her family and friends,' Prince William chipped in. 'We just want you to have an awesome time and enjoy the line-up.'

Harry stepped up to the mike again: 'When William and I first had the idea, we forgot we would end up standing here desperately trying to think of something funny to say. We'll leave that to the funny people – and Ricky Gervais.'

Among the audience listening on the radio was Harry's Household Cavalry squadron who were serving in Iraq: 'I wish I was there with you,' Harry told them. 'I'm sorry I can't be. But to all of those on operations at the moment, we'd both like to say – stay safe.'

The Princes looked to be enjoying themselves as much as anyone else, not least their girlfriends: Kate Middleton sitting with her sister Pippa and parents Michael and Carol; while Chelsy Davy and Harry were openly affectionate. Everyone in the Royal Box entered into the spirit of the proceedings, taking part in Mexican waves, holding their arms aloft to Rod Stewart's 'Sailing', joining in the mass singalong for Take That's 'Back For Good', and dancing to 'Maneater' by Nelly Furtado.

Fittingly, the Princes introduced Duran Duran, famously one of their mother's favourite bands. Simon Le Bon and co returned the compliment by playing 'Rio' in memory of 'this country's favourite princess.' It was a roll call of the greats: Elton John started the proceedings with 'Your Song' and was also the last on stage, with 'Saturday Night's Alright For Fighting', 'Tiny Dancer' and 'Are You Ready For Love?' Lily Allen was there, singing 'Smile' and 'LDN', while there was a medley of Andrew Lloyd Webber numbers with Josephs old and new – Donny Osmond, Jason Donovan and Lee Mead – singing 'Any Dream Will Do'. P Diddy was there, too: he sang the song 'Missing You', written in the wake of the death of Notorious B.I.G., who died in 1997, the same year as Diana. 'We miss you, our princess,' he said. Even Simon Cowell dropped the familiar Mr Nasty act, telling Wills and Harry how well they'd done: 'You have put on one heck of a show,' he said. 'In years to come, if you ever get tired of running the country, you can come and work for me producing TV shows.'

In other words, this was the concert of the year, filled to the brim with show business royalty so it was fitting that Tom had top billing. Despite living in the States, he increasingly appeared to be a part of the very fabric of British popular life. His popularity was only growing these days: after his performance at the Concert For Diana and speaking out about Welsh workers losing their jobs, the affection the British public held him in was palpable. If not physically, he had certainly spiritually come home.

Yet the other side of his life was very much in evidence, too. In December 2007, a boxing match was staged between Ricky Hatton and Floyd

Mayweather Jr in Las Vegas: this was, of course, one of the places in the world that Tom knew best. And so, fittingly, Tom was asked to sing the British national anthem at the MGM Grand before the fight began. In the meantime, a whole host of fellow A-listers, including Becks (the Spice Girls were performing in Las Vegas at the time), Michael Jordan, Jack Nicholson, Sylvester Stallone, Jude Law, Wesley Snipes, Kevin Bacon, Denzel Washington, Will Ferrell, P Diddy and 50 Cent were in town to see how it all went. In the event, Hatton lost, and British fans were widely considered to have disgraced themselves, booing during the singing of the American national anthem. It caused widespread comment and considerable embarrassment back home.

Even so, it did not put Tom off attending boxing matches. In early 2008, there was a match between Joe Calzaghe, a fellow Welshman, and the American Bernard Hopkins, slugging it out for the Light Heavyweight World Championship, again in Las Vegas. This really brought the celebrity brigade out in force: Tom was there, plus fellow Welsh stars Catherine Zeta Jones and Ioan Gruffudd, as well as Brits Cat Deeley and Simon Cowell. America was represented by, among others, Brad Pitt, Whitney Houston, Bruce Willis and Pete Sampras. Tom sang the Welsh national anthem, and this time the crowd did not disgrace itself. Calzaghe won.

The Welsh connection reared its head in an altogether more unlikely way halfway through 2008. A new singing sensation had arrived on the music scene in the form of Aimee Anne Duffy, more commonly known just as Duffy, from Nefyn in Gwynedd. Duffy had a powerful singing voice, so much so that rumours sprang up that she was, in fact, Tom's child. This was totally untrue as her father is John Duffy. 'I'm dealing with this every day here,' said Duffy, of the gossip that was sweeping America. 'It's kind of bizarre. You've got to laugh. He [John] is such a sweet guy. He runs a pub and is so traditional. I don't know if he's read the accusations about potential fatherhood.'

It was certainly a little unusual to be accused of fathering a child on the sole basis that you share the same nationality, but Tom took it in good stead. Indeed, he even talked about doing some work with her, citing her as a potential fellow singer on an upcoming album of duets. 'That's because she's Welsh and she can sing, not just because she's Welsh,' he said. 'I'd like to do something with her.' The music industry thought it would be a good match: 'She'd be great alongside Tom,' said a source. 'He's the king of re-invention and she's very much the girl of the moment. Both have incredible voices, both are Welsh – it's a match made in Heaven.'

Tom, of course, was also very much of the moment, but then he had been by this stage for a good forty years. He was reminded of the early days when a collection of 1,850 songs and musical arrangements came up for auction at the Idea Generation gallery in London. Dating from the early 1960s, this included work, some previously unreleased, by the likes of Tom, David Bowie, Jimmy Page and Gene Vincent. They had belonged to the record producer Joe Meek, who kept the collection on quarter inch tapes in tea boxes. Meek himself had long since died, having shot his landlady in 1967 and then killing himself. Cliff Cooper bought the tapes for £300 from Meek's estate, which turned out to be a good investment, given that they were now estimated as being worth about £250,000.

Tom had visited Joe's studio in 1963, when he was working under the name Tommy Scott and the Senators: two numbers from those sessions were now up for grabs. But Tom and Joe had not hit it off. 'Tom and Joe, who was gay, never got on,' Ken Ledran, chairman of the Joe Meek Society revealed. Nick Moran, who has made a film about Meek, called *Telstar*, recounted how when Joe made a pass at Tom, 'Tom punched him. I know, because Tom told me when I was doing research for the movie. Mind you, Joe did try to fight back.'

He certainly hadn't got the measure of Tom. Tom was now beginning to look back on a lifetime of wine, women and song, and that was reflected in his latest album, *24 Hours,* which contained his *mea culpa* to Linda, 'The Road'. 'It's about how my road always leads back to her,' said Tom. 'She may not have liked some of the things I did, but I could not be apart.' The secret behind the marriage that often perplexed the world was laid bare again: 'Linda wouldn't say to me, "What do you mean by that?" he said. 'No, she wouldn't do that. The thing she likes best is, "But the road always leads back to you". And that's the truth. I will never leave my wife. It never entered my mind. We are still in love with one another. You know, we're not sexually like we were, but we are still in tune with one another, we can still have fun with one another, we still talk. She's still the Welsh girl I married.'

An understanding had grown up between the two of them over the years, too. Tom related one incident which, more than anything, gave an insight into their home life. 'We were having a bit of a barney one night in LA – sometimes it can start off really nice, a nice dinner, back to the music room, put on the old records that we used to dance to when we were teenagers, and it's all lovely, lovely, lovely,' he recalled. 'And then it becomes, "Well, what about when you did this?" [referring to other women] So she said: "Let me tell you something but you've got to stand there and you've got to promise me that you will not try and get hold of me." I thought, "Jesus, what's she going to tell me?" I'm expecting the worst and we're both well oiled by this point. She says: "If you couldn't sing, you wouldn't have a friend in the world," and runs out of the room. Well, I fell on the floor in a heap. She thought that was the worst thing she could ever say to me – I thought it was hilarious.'

For all that Linda thought she was goading him, it was also a sign of a relationship that had endured a very long time. Unlike all the other women he had met along the way, only Linda knew Tom as the miner's boy from the valleys, the young man he once had been. Only she could remember him before the fame and the fortune, the wealth and the acclaim. And the fact that she had become attached to him back then, long before they had a large mansion with a music room and a lifestyle that would have been inconceivable in their younger days that proved to him that it was Tom the man she wanted, not Tom the star. Something between them had never changed since those early days, another of the reasons that the marriage had endured.

The album might have been a reflection on the past, but it was also yet another example of Tom's astonishing ability to reinvent himself, always managing to stay one step ahead of the crowd. The producers were Future Cuts, who had worked with Lily Allen and Kate Nash, and one of the songs, 'Sugar Daddy', had been written for Tom by Bono and The Edge. Bono was to duet with Tom on the number and sounded thoroughly excited by it all, 'I'd see Tom Jones on Saturday night on a variety show – I must have been, like, eight years old – and he's sweating and he's an animal and he's unrestrained. He has a big black voice in a white guy.'

Indeed, it was largely down to Bono that the album had been made at all. The two had met in a nightclub in Dublin and got chatting, and the project really took off. 'Well, he sort of sparked me up to get involved in songwriting,' Tom related. 'We were just talking and I said, "I'd love you to write me a song" and he replied, "Yeah, OK, so long as it's about you and not just another song". He asked me what it was like in Wales, how I came into showbusiness, how I felt with the gear on. I said, "I've got the shoes, I've got what it takes, I've got it". I also said, "You're gonna get your hands dirty when you're digging a ditch." Those words duly appeared in the finished number.

Bono wrote the song, recorded a version of it himself and sent it to Tom. 'Bono tries to sound like me on it,' said Tom, who was clearly delighted by the whole thing. 'He told me, "I was trying to do my best Tom Jones impression". I said, "It's great". When I recorded it with Future Cut, we'd send it back and forth to Bono and let him have a listen. He loves it and is very complimentary. It was great working with him... I told Bono, "I'm not a sugar daddy!" He told me it was a cheeky, ballsy thing and not to be taken literally.'

It was his first solo album of new material in 15 years and Tom cited Amy Winehouse as an influence: 'We've been thinking of this for a while, doing a retro sound, but new,' he said. 'And Amy Winehouse, she cracked it ... the fire is still in me. I want to be a contender.' He still was.

So was his voice. With any singer, there's the concern that as he or she grows older, the voice will suffer, but in Tom's case, this was not happening. His vocal ability had changed slightly, but it was as strong as it had ever been. 'Yes, it's in great shape, only lost a little top, like everybody,' he told one interviewer. 'When you're young, your voice is higher and as you get older, it goes down. I've only lost a tone off my top. I used to hit Cs very easily, now it's B flat, but my lower register is much richer. What you lose on the swings, you gain on the roundabouts. I love to sing as much as I ever did, maybe even more so now. When you're young, you're on fire but I was always trying to top the last thing I sang. As the years have gone on, I've read more into the songs rather than just attack stuff.'

When the album was released, it garnered extremely positive reviews – marred only slightly by internet reports that Tom, aged 68 at the time, had met an untimely demise. His own repost to this came soon after in November 2008, when he opened a new show at the MGM Grand Theatre in Las Vegas with the song 'I'm Alive'. 'I read my own obituary' he explained. A friend had told him what was being said. Fellow Las Vegas performer Cook E Jarr then left a message on Tom's answerphone saying, 'I don't want to stay on this planet if something's happened to you.' Tom was, in fact, in rude health, back on stage and fizzing over with energy. Much of the new show was made up of material from the new album: the audience loved what they heard, especially 'I'm Alive', the opening track on the new album. 'The song shows that I'll walk on,' Tom affirmed. 'I'll keep going and not just reflect on the seasons of my life. I'm not in the autumn yet.'

You could say that again. The same month, Tom took on a challenge that would have been difficult for a man half his age. *The Culture Show* on BBC Two got him and a Welsh male voice choir to compete with one another – busking. The idea was to see who could raise more for charity: a microphone and speakers was set up on the South Bank of the Thames near the Royal Festival Hall: by the time Tom appeared, a crowd of four hundred had gathered. 'Can you hear me all right?' he asked, and got a massive cheer for his pains, before launching into, 'Put on your red dress, baby, cause we're going out tonight.'

This was actually a huge deal. Tom's stature was

such that he might easily have disdained a project of this nature: it had all the possibility of blowing up in his face, which for a star of his magnitude would have been appalling embarrassing – after all, no other big name was out singing on the Embankment that night. People could have jeered, treated it only as a stunt, or worse still, not shown up at all. Instead, Tom's natural exuberance and bonhomie managed to make it an occasion to remember: he pulled it off with finesse.

It was one of his more unusual performances, but the audience loved it. Champagne buckets were passed round to collect money from on-lookers. Tom spied a £5 note. 'That's more than I got paid for my first gig,' he observed. He launched into 'Green, Green Grass of Home', followed by 'Whole Lotta Shakin' Going On' and 'Great Balls of Fire': originally he had been scheduled to sing just three numbers, but increased this to six – and then sang them twice. 'You ought to do this professionally and give up the busking!' shouted one member of the audience, before everyone erupted into cheers for 'It's Not Unusual'. In the event, Tom beat the rival choir – and raised £460 for charity.

In January, 2009, Tom unveiled a whole new look. For the first time, he was willing to allow his audience to see him as he really was – with grey hair, which was shortly to turn a snowy white. The new look was revealed at a performance in Las Vegas: 'I am sorry, I just didn't have time to dye it before the performance,' he told the surprised audience, but if truth be told, there was more to it than this. Tom was finally willing to look his age. He had spent a career defying the years, but the urge to do so simply wasn't there any more: Tom was in his late sixties, and he was happy to admit to it. Why not? What more did he have to prove? Indeed, given all the plastic surgery he'd had in the past and despite his great fame, this was possibly the first time he really was telling the world to take him on his own terms.

Indeed, he was pretty open about everything he'd had done, too. 'The first thing I had done when I started to make money was have my teeth capped 'cause they were in bad shape,' he said. 'Then I had my nose fixed because it was broken through all the fights I'd had. Then a lot later I had some fat taken out from under my chin – hence the goatee. I haven't had my face pulled or anything. The guy I saw in LA said you've got to be careful. You want to look like you. Every Christmas I take five weeks off and stop dyeing my hair. It used to come out as a dirty grey, but this year it was more white and it looked pretty good. So for my first engagement I tried it out and people were shouting, "You look great, Tom." So I thought, thank God, now I don't have to dye it any more.'

He didn't need to. In the early days, he had to make the best of himself because there was everything to play for, and while the voice itself was enough to move mountains, there was no harm in presenting a good looking package, too. Tom might have had the talent, but he certainly backed it up with the appearance. He was never going to leave anything to chance. But now, he could relax, enjoy and be himself. He was too old to be the thrusting young stud he had once appeared as –

but he didn't need to anymore. He was the grand old man of pop. The granddaddy of the current generation who could still give the young upstarts something to live up to – which they had to work very hard to achieve.

That said, Tom wasn't exactly underrating himself. One newspaper ran a series about sexy songs, and if there was one person in the country who knew about the seductive powers of music, it was Mr Sex Bomb himself. 'I've always been aware of my sexiness, and the fact that my singing was sexy, ever since I was a little boy, liking girls – either you have it in your tone or you don't,' he said. Tom had always had 'it', no matter whether he was a young lad from the valleys singing his heart out in a pub, or a superstar entertaining a stadium of fans.

'If you have an appealing tone, it can sound sexy. Like Barry White – he had a very sexy tone. If you are trying to seduce someone you should use a ballad. You want a song that is, well, sad is the wrong word, but emotional – an emotional ballad. My seduction song would be '(It Looks Like) I'll Never Fall in Love Again'. Women have told me they go weak at the knees when I sing that.'

In May 2009, a new uber-luxury hotel, the Mardan Palace Hotel opened in Antalya, Turkey. Tom was one of a host of celebrities asked to perform, and his fee, for less than an hour, was a cool £1 million, the same amount commanded by that relative newcomer Mariah Carey. The hotel opening was a massive event and attracted the most glittering of the A-listers: fellow invitees included Sharon Stone and Richard Gere. Tom was, as always, right at home. But his versatility and breadth of appeal meant he was also much in demand elsewhere. Tom also turned up to perform at Glastonbury that summer, proof, if it were needed, that he was just as popular among the younger generation as he had ever been, which was one of the secrets behind the longevity of his career. His appeal was not one-dimensional: it spanned generations. Jones the Voice was loved by everyone, young and old.

In June 2009, a return to Britain really did beckon. Tom would be the first to admit to having a great time in the States, but he was getting older now, and it was becoming clear – not least through how much he was doing in and for Wales – that he was beginning to think it was time to go home. 'I've had a great time living in LA but after all these years we think now is the time to move home,' said Tom. 'My wife Linda's been getting homesick lately and we have been talking it over for a while. I decided to move before Robbie [Williams] but he got here before me. I said to him, "I've been talking about it all this time and you've gone and done it!" Britain has always been home. I love coming here and miss it more and more when I go back to LA. It's the people and humour you can't get anywhere else. We'd like somewhere in the country, but I think we'll get a place in London first to ease back into it.'

So it had some full circle. Jones the Voice was now show business aristocracy Sir Tom Jones. And no one could doubt he had deserved it. Tom has given joy to millions; one of the most popular, best-loved and outstanding talents of his generation. He was finishing where he had started out, in the country that had made him a star. Welcome back to Britain, and above all to Wales – Sir Tom Jones.

CHAPTER 15

NEW HORIZONS

On 7 June 2010 Sir Tom Jones turned 70 and to mark the occasion he signed a £1.5 million contract with Island Records – and promptly landed right in the middle of a new controversy. He was due to release a new album, *Praise & Blame,* that year, his 39th to date and a record that was to be a 'deeply personal' collection of gospel melodies reflecting on the great man's take on life so far, but David Sharpe, vice president of the Island Records label, loathed it. In a leaked email he demanded, 'I have just listened to the album and want to know if this is some sick joke? We did not invest a fortune in an established artist for him to deliver 12 tracks from the common book of prayer [sic]. This is certainly not what we paid for.'

This was no way to talk about a superstar. Tom was livid. 'People are going to read this and think the record company doesn't like this or that I've made a mistake,' he told the *Western Mail.* 'It's not coming from the creative people in the record company, because they're backing it up all the way. I mean, they're thrilled with it, so I don't understand it. When I questioned them and said, "What the hell is this all about? Who is this fella?" I don't even know who he is, I found out that he's some fella who signs cheques or something. But he's not in the creative side of it and they're 100% behind it, but people don't know that. In the press it says that I've gone off and made something that the record company didn't pay me for and that they don't like it. People tell me that all publicity is good publicity, that's what I've been told. People say to me, "Well, it's being talked about", but to me it's being talked about in a negative way. Hopefully, if there's any good that comes out of it, it's that people will wonder about [the new album]. But it isn't the way I would handle it by going and making a stupid statement. That's not going to help it.

'They've apologised, they can't apologise enough – and they've said "We'll make good on this".'

It had clearly hurt his feelings but Tom had sold about 100 million records by that stage so he could afford to shrug it off. A single from the forthcoming album, a cover of the John Lee Hooker classic, 'Burning Hell', was due to be released to coincide with his birthday. He appeared on the penultimate episode of *Friday Night with Jonathan Ross*, performing the number and shortly afterwards had the satisfaction of seeing his album debut at number two on the British album chart. Vindication, if it were needed, that he remained an enormously popular singer and that the public loved what he did.

Praise & Blame was a reference to Tom's past

life, a life he freely admitted had been a little rackety at times. 'I've been praised throughout my career, and I've been blamed for things, too,' he told the *Guardian*. 'Well, you know, maybe my pants were a little too tight. Maybe they were. And the knicker-throwing. As if I'd instigated it. I didn't start it. But once things happen, you try and turn it around to your advantage.'

It soon became clear just why Tom had been so hurt: the album was one of the most personal he had ever made. What started out as a putative Christmas album had turned into something much more: 'We said, "If we're going to do this, why don't we take a bit of time and get it done right?"' he said. 'And it was suggested that we approach the producer Ethan Johns. I'd heard of him. I knew who his father was. And he said, "I like it to be real, we pick the songs, get in the studio, get in there with a rhythm section and try them out." And I said, "Well, that sounds good to me."'

The first two songs they picked were 'Did Trouble Me' and the gospel number, 'Run On', and the latter shaped the rest of the album. 'Suddenly it happened,' said Tom. 'It caught fire. We thought, "Let's look for some spiritual things, uplifting things, things that mean something." And they have to be strong when you've only got a rhythm section, they have to speak for themselves, really. And so we got to the recording studio and said, "Well, how do we treat this?" Song by song.'

It seemed apt, somehow, at this stage in his career that he was looking at spiritual matters – the knicker-throwing days were now well and truly in the past.

And anyway, the critics enjoyed it. Andrew Perry in the *Daily Telegraph* said it was 'by far Jones's best album in two decades ... with its loose, spontaneous sound, and the all-pervasive sense of artistic rebirth, it's a revelation.' Rick Moore, writing in *American Songwriter,* said that 'on this excellent collection of songs examining the human condition, Jones confronts the issues of heaven and hell in a way that Cash did for much of his life, especially toward the end of it... Jones and Johns have made a real statement in the same way that Rubin, and of course T. Bone Burnett, do almost every time they produce an album.' That was high praise indeed and somewhat justified Tom's remark about David Sharpe's comments coming from someone who was not involved in the creative side.

And they were not alone. 'Overall, it's an extraordinary achievement: *Praise & Blame* represents the kind of reconnection with his core creative fire that was hinted on a few tracks of his last album, *24 Hours,* but is here left naked and bleeding raw, bereft of showbiz blandishments,' wrote Andy Gill in the *Independent.*

'[It] conveys the contrition of a sinner as he delivers a mixture of traditional spirituals and contemporary gospel songs tautly arranged for a small band,' was how Stephen Holden put it in *The New York Times.* 'It is a respectful, expressively focused exploration of a genre beloved by Mr Jones's American counterpart, Elvis Presley.'

Michael Hann in the *Guardian* said, 'at last Jones the artist is the match of Jones the entertainer,' while Allison Stewart, writing in the *Washington Post*, opined that *Praise & Blame* is 'Jones's "O Brother", "Raising Sand" and "Ain't No Grave" all rolled into one, a mixed bag of roots-related styles – blues, gospel-lite, country-folk, rockabilly, soul – stripped of all fat and reduced to the barest elements of voice and spartan, if often electrified, instrumentation. The song choices are impeccable, from a thunderous cover of Bob Dylan's *Oh Mercy* standout, "What Good Am I?" to a holy roller redo of John Lee Hooker's "Burning Hell", all propelled by Jones's remarkable voice, still a marvel of quaveriness and bluster and sinew after all these years.' And so there it was – both a critical and commercial success.

He was certainly in as much demand as ever, performing in September at a Help for Heroes charity concert at Twickenham Stadium and shortly afterwards pitching up on the other side of the pond to appear on the *Late Show with David Letterman* in New York. He was the subject of a BBC documentary series, *Imagine,* too (the second Welsh singer in a matter of months after Dame Shirley Bassey), presented by the cerebral Alan Yentob and entitled, somewhat self-effacingly, *What Good Am I?* 'Very' would seem to be the answer, but viewers were presented with a somewhat more thoughtful Tom than they had previously become used to seeing. Again the subject of Tom as sex symbol came up, an image that had in some ways obscured the true depth of his talent – 'I've only got myself to blame. The pants were tight,' said Tom. 'I thought I was a young, virile, no bullshit artist. But maybe I was exploiting the sexual part of it. Once you start to undo buttons and girls scream then you tend to open another one. I didn't know it was going to catch up with me.'

His friendship with Elvis featured, along with a frank admittance that his marriage to Linda had had its rocky moments: 'We had a few blow-ups and she would explode, rightfully so. But it was all part and parcel of the thing, I felt.' And again the story was told of how Tom's son Mark had rescued his father when his career seemed to falter – Mark 'wanted to shift the focus of attention three feet upwards.' It was a mark of Tom's stature that he was afforded this treatment – Yentob has a very serious reputation, interested more by the higher arts. But Tom was now a part of the cultural landscape, his contribution to the modern-day cultural scene in Britain incalculable.

More details of Tom's past emerged in various forms. Roger Dinham, a careers advisor at the Jobcentre in Pontypridd in Wales, ruefully reflected that his advice to Tom to take a job in a local gelatin factory had not been up to the mark: 'He said he didn't want it because he was going to be a pop star and he was going to make it in music. I said I didn't care and he should get his backside down the factory,' he recalled. 'But I'm a fan and I'm glad he ignored my advice.'

In fact, recently discovered employment records dating back to the early 1960s, just before Tom made it, show that his name cropped up quite regularly at that time – or at least the name Thomas John Woodward did. One stated he only wanted something that wouldn't 'dirty his fingernails'.

Another said, 'He does not want shift work but I believe the reason for his not liking shifts is because he is a member of a vocal group which is supposedly an amateur affair. From the number of adverts one sees in the local press, however, it seems that this group has a good thing going. From the way he is able to dress, it would seem that Mr Woodward's little hobby is highly lucrative and this would also account for his non-enthusiasm in securing employment.'

A further record said, 'Claimant showed me a letter from Decca Studios confirming a recording session had been arranged. He has been talking about "going professional" since April but he is still signing the UR [Unemployment Register] and not autograph books.'

Not for much longer, though – a massive star was about to be born.

'They are a wonderful look at the beginning of a glittering career when Tom Jones was trying to make a living from his singing,' said Richard Westwood Brookes from Mullock's Auctions in Shropshire, which was selling the records. 'There are also some quite acerbic and sarcastic remarks made by the civil servants about him. The records set quite a scene with attractive Tom Jones in his tight trousers and smart clothes on one side of the desk and the civil servant on the other.'

All vintage Tom, but throughout 2010 he continued to remain in the news. He might have been the grand old man of the pop music scene – there was some amusement when ft emerged that his backstage demands these days amounted simply to an iron and a plentiful supply of black towels – but it was certainly not holding him back nor denting his popularity. In the year before he had turned 70, the Hungarian magazine *Periodika* voted him the Sexiest Man in the World. Then the year itself kicked off with a rather saucy observation from his band of nearly 50 years previously, The Senators, to the effect that they had never been paid for songs, including 'Little Lonely One', 'That's What We'll Do', 'Lonely Joe' and 'I Was A Fool', to which Tom's management countered neither had Tom. 'We never received any royalties,' he said.

On 26 September 2010 Tom appeared on Radio 4's *Desert Island Discs*, where he appeared to admit to something of a wild life: 'I did feel like [I had] that,' he told presenter Kirsty Young, while choosing a bucket and spade as his luxury and nominating Jerry Lee Lewis's 'Whole Lotta Shakin' Goin' On' as his favourite number. 'I've always tried to rein myself in but sometimes things got the better of me. I've only myself to blame. "Sex Bomb", you can't get away from that title. When you do things, sometimes you create a monster without actually realising. Sometimes I should rein myself in a little bit.' But he did add that he and Linda were still very much in love: 'She's still the Welsh girl I married,' he said.

The normally imperturbable Kirsty seemed to have been quite overwhelmed by the experience. 'I was grateful that I was interviewing him in the autumn of his years, because God knows if he had walked into my studio 30 years ago I would not have been responsible for my actions,' she told the *Guardian*. 'He pulsates sexuality. It is unfair. He has an animal magnetism and he is very at home with himself. I can only imagine he is a killer in the sack.' Young was far from being alone in those sentiments. Her fellow presenter Cat Deeley also confided, 'Tom Jones does something weird to me. He'll go, "I'm looking at you," and I can feel it when he does.'

Indeed much of the country felt the same. In the summer of 2011, Tom appeared at T in the Park, one of the most popular acts who played there despite being about 50 years older than most of the other attendees. That same year he was a guest vocalist on Hugh Laurie's debut album, *Let Them Talk*, and the duo performed together in New Orleans, something that appeared on the ITV series *Perspectives*. This was followed up by an appearance on *American Idol*. He was more in demand than ever. However, even Tom was human: he was forced to cancel a concert in Monaco in August 2011 because of what was initially thought to be a heart scare but later turned out to be an extreme case of dehydration. It was severe enough for him to be hospitalised, although he was duly released and able to start touring again.

Tom continued to find new audiences, and did so again when in October 2011 it was announced that he'd signed up to be a judge on the television reality show *The Voice*, a somewhat appropriate name given that he himself had often been known as 'Tom the Voice', back in his native Wales. He was to be working alongside Jessie J and Danny O'Donoghue (who was picked in preference to Will Young, causing something of a row) on the popular show, presented by Holly Willoughby and Reggie Yates. The concept was to pick acts solely on the basis of their singing ability.

'This is a strong show,' said Tom. 'It's all about talent – but it's also exciting, competitive and compelling television. I've been blessed over the years to share the stage with some of the world's finest artists, and I look forward to being part of the team that discovers a great, new genuine talent.'

The Voice was based on a Dutch concept in which four superstar 'coaches' worked with a series of competitors in order to find a major new talent – exactly the kind of reality show that had proven extremely popular with viewers who enjoyed *Britain's Got Talent* and *The X Factor*. The USP in this case being that it was the voice alone that was important and nothing else. It kicked off with a so-called 'Blind Audition' in which the judges listened to the competitors with their backs turned; if a judge decided he or she wanted that competitor on their team, they pressed a red button and their chair would swivel round.

If more than one judge wanted the same competitor, then the competitor got to choose the person they wanted to go with. This continued until each coach had 12 people on their team, at which point team members were required to compete with each other; losing team members could also be poached by other coaches and so the process would go on until the teams were down to eight. After this the show moved to the round called 'The Knockouts' and then ulti-mately three live shows to find the winner, who would secure a contract with Universal Music.

The Voice began to air in 2012, the same year that Tom released his next album, *Spirit In The Room*. His appearance was beginning to change: gone was the black hair and in its place a shock of white, complemented by a neat little beard. He was now seemingly the elder statesman to both the pop industry and also his fellow judges on the show. Tom was rather enjoying the fact that a new crowd was now taking an interest in him. 'Yes, there were some kids who wanted a photo when I flew in from LA last week,' he told *GQ*. 'I know that when we were talking about putting the judges together they wanted a cross-section of people. They've got me there because I've been around so long, but it's nice to know that the kids are taking notice not just [of] Jessie J, and Danny O'Donoghue. That's nice. That's flattering.'

He was also enjoying the show, something that was a totally new direction for him. 'This is the first time I've ever been involved in something that's not just about me,' he continued. 'Over my career, all the decisions I've had to make about song choices and producers were all about my next record. Now I'm trying to pass that onto other people. That's new – you're throwing yourself out there. When I was watching the blind audition shows back, I noticed that there's a girl on show three who's singing great and none of us turned around! The viewing audience must have thought there was something wrong with us. The thing is, at first they were calling me "trigger happy" because as soon as someone started singing I'd be hitting the button. The producers told us we had to slow down because we had a lot of people to listen to and we could only choose ten people. You can't explain all that to the contestants or to the viewers!'

The line-up of coaches was to change over the next few years, although Tom remained a constant, and he became part of the overall soap opera that surrounds such shows, telling everyone he would miss Jessie and Danny when they left, while welcoming on board newbies Kylie Minogue, Rita Ora and Ricky Wilson and generally behaving like the affable elder statesmen he had clearly come to be.

'The more you do it, the easier it gets,' he told *Unreality TV* a couple of years in. 'You are more accustomed to it. For the first series, it is new territory and you are feeling your way through. The second is easier than the first and by the third time you are more familiar with what you are doing. Am I more relaxed this time? Yes, definitely, but you still have to learn to say "no" in a way that doesn't hurt or deflate the contestant.'

He was certainly kinder than some reality show judges in that respect.

That blind audition was more difficult for the judges than it sounded. 'I go on my instinct and what I hear,' Tom continued. 'That's all you have to go on. You don't know whether it is a boy, girl, man or woman. It could be a boy with a high voice that sounds like a girl. You don't know until you turn around what you are going to see.'

Tom also confessed that he wasn't always able to build the team he wanted. 'It is frustrating when some good ones slip away,' he went on. 'There are some people I would have liked. But it is their decision to make and they will have a great experience with any one of the other coaches, no matter who they go with.' But he must have been doing something right: in the first series he coached Leanne Mitchell, who went on to win the competition. The two of them sang 'Mama Told Me Not To Come', one of Tom's earlier hits. In later series, the format was tweaked slightly, cutting back on the number of live shows and – in series three – bringing in new presenters in the shape of Emma Willis and Marvin Humes, with Zoe Ball stepping in for the live shows. Tom, along with Will.i.am, remained a constant.

It was hard to escape the conclusion that he was very much looking back on his life at the time, though. As the senior judge on a show that nurtured up-and-coming talent, Tom wouldn't have been human if he hadn't indulged in the odd moment of retrospection and it might have been in an acknowledgement of his roots that he took a highly unusual decision when it came to launching his next single. As a boy he used to go into Cardiff to a shop called Spillers Records; founded in 1894, the store was listed in the Guinness World Records as the oldest record shop in the world. But it had been having problems: in 2006 it faced closure and was saved only by a local campaign fronted by the Manic Street Preachers; in 2011 it was forced to move from its home in The Hayes to Morgan Arcade.

It was thus in a display of loyalty to his childhood haunt that Tom's latest single, 'Evil', a number he made with former White Stripes frontman Jack

241

White, first appeared in a limited edition of 100 three-coloured vinyls at £15 each, available only from Spillers. The fans flocked. 'It's been quite overwhelming – we've had people from all over the country and Europe ringing up about the release,' said a slightly flabbergasted Ashli Todd, owner of the shop. The single later went on sale nationwide.

Spirit In The Room, an album of covers of songs by artists including Paul McCartney, Paul Simon, Leonard Cohen, Richard and Linda Thompson, Blind Willie Johnson, Tom Waits and The Low Anthem, came out; this was followed shortly after by a bravura performance at the Queen's Diamond Jubilee Concert. Performing alongside the likes of Sir Elton John, Dame Shirley Bassey, Robbie Williams, Kylie Minogue and other A-list names too numerous to mention, Tom belted out 'Mama Told Me Not To Come' and 'Delilah'. The night was universally acknowledged to be a magical one, with the 86-year-old monarch beaming at the assembled crowds and Prince Charles praising his mother – and getting the crowd to cheer for his father, Prince Philip, who was in hospital at the time.

Tom's enduring popularity ensured that he remained a constant at festivals, appreciated also by a new audience who had been introduced to him courtesy of *The Voice*. August 2012 saw him appear at the V Festival in Weston Park: he flew in on the Capital One helicopter, looking every inch the silver fox, dapper in black and exuding charisma. 'The veteran perma-tanned crooner, whose distinctive earthy tones retain their ability to seamlessly cut across genres, styles and form,

draws across a wide spectrum of his back catalogue,' wrote *VirtualFestivals.com*. 'Emerging into
bright sunlight sporting a high-collared black
frockcoat that gives him the appearance of a dys-
topian future vicar, Jones displays throughout an
effortless crowd control and showmanship; commanding his flock with a flicker of an eyebrow, a
beamingly knowing flash of his pearly whites or
his sincere and heartfelt gratitude between songs
for such a rapturous reception.'

'Rapturous' was the word for it: the crowd loved
Tom, as indeed did the nation. Not so much sex
bomb these days as national treasure, his popularity had never been greater than now. He was
more than holding his own with the younger acts
– if anything they were spurring him on. And this
appearance was followed up shortly after by
headlining at Radio 2's Live in Hyde Park festival.

Tom had got to the stage of his life where he was
being recognised by many organisations far and
wide for his contribution to society. He was given
a Lifetime Achievement Award at a Nordoff
Robbins Silver Clef event; the charity provides
music therapy for children with special needs. He
then came top of a poll conducted by the Campaign for Real Ale (CAMRA) as the star most
people would like to have a pint with, coming in
just ahead of Robbie Williams – ironic really, as
Tom prefers champagne and Robbie doesn't drink
at all. 'I'm in Los Angeles soon, so I'm going to see
if Tom is free to hook up for a barbecue,' Tom
Jones's fellow judge Danny O'Donoghue told *OK!*
Magazine. 'I went out drinking with him once
until 7am. He loves champagne. I asked him why

and he said, "I used to drink beer and put on weight, so I went to vodkas and got so drunk I kept getting into fights".'

But Tom had been around for a long time now. Perhaps it was this sense of nearing an end that had him in reflective mode: in 2014, he made it clear that despite having lived in Los Angeles since 1974, he wanted to be buried in his home town of Pontypridd. 'All my forefathers are there,' he explained.

But he was still performing as much as ever, in 2014 appearing at the final of ten British Summer Time shows in Hyde Park and prompting specu-lation that his late-flowering television career was actually having a positive impact on his live shows.

'People tend to forget that "the Voice" was Jones's nickname long before a TV show of that title was devised,' wrote David Sinclair in a review in *The Times*. 'But for all his much-vaunted ability, the singer from Pontypridd has taken some ques-tionable artistic turns during a career that for many years found him sidelined as a Las Vegas cabaret turn. An unintended consequence of his tenure as a TV talent show judge seems to be that, at the age of 74, he has become more rigorous in selecting songs that match his own strengths and disposition as a singer.'

He garnered similar praise for a concert at Edinburgh Castle: 'There are few pop performers who manage to achieve near-complete career re-newal as they hit their 70th year, but with 2010's rich blues odyssey *Praise & Blame*, Tom Jones broke that particular mould,' wrote David Pollock in the *Independent*. 'His previous appearance at one of Edinburgh Castle's showpiece summer concerts in the amphitheatre, normally used for the Military Tattoo, was a play-the-hits round of satisfied expectations. This time – and to the credit of Jones, his well-drilled band and a musical director who deserves huge praise for the whole endeavour – the hits were thoroughly trotted out, but with a musical depth and playfulness which suggested that Jones isn't afraid to push at the boundaries of his fans' demands.'

It was to be a busy summer – from there Tom was off to the Belladrum Tartan Heart festival, near Beauly, Inverness-shire.

There was a rare frisson of negativity in the summer of 2014 when it was suggested that 'Delilah' should no longer be traditionally sung before every Wales rugby international on the grounds that it trivialised violence towards women. This briefly became a real issue: Dafydd Iwan, former president of Plaid Cymru, the Welsh nationalist party, said, 'Do we really realise what we are singing about here? It is a song about murder and it does tend to trivialise the idea of murdering a woman. It's a pity these words now have been elevated to the status of a secondary national anthem.'

But the Welsh Rugby Union disagreed: 'Within rugby, "Delilah" has gained prominence through its musicality rather than because of its lyrics,' said a spokesman. 'There is, however, plenty of precedent in art and literature, prominently in Shakespearean tragedies, for instance, for negative aspects of life to be portrayed.'

Tom was a little disgusted by the suggestion. 'I

245

love to hear "Delilah" being sung at the Welsh games and it makes me very proud to be Welsh,' he told the *Daily Mirror*. 'If they're looking into the lyrics, it's not a political statement. It's something that happens in life. That this woman was unfaithful to him and he just loses it. But the great thing about the song, the thing that everyone picks up on, is the chorus. I don't think they are thinking about the lyrics and I wasn't thinking as the man killing the girl when I was singing it. If it's going to be taken literally like that it takes the fun out of it.'

And so the debate raged on.

It has been an extraordinary life, this journey from an impoverished childhood in the Welsh valleys to international superstardom, but Tom's appeal has merely grown over the years. He may be older now, but the twinkle is still there in his eye, the Voice (his own, *not* the television programme) as rich and strong as ever, as well as the kind of popularity that only decades in the public eye can bring. Tom's marriage to Linda has endured. As for *The Voice* (the television programme, *not* his own), it may yet endure.

'I'd like to think it can go on for as long as *The X Factor* or *Strictly* and be on TV for more than a decade,' said Tom. 'But it's up to the public how long it goes on for. It's not our call as coaches. It will continue if it's popular enough and people like it. It's about keeping the show fresh and that's a lot to do with the talent. The feedback I get from people is great. I don't get any negativity whatsoever. People tell me they love the show. I even get kids who know who I am now. They know me because of *The Voice* and that's a flattering feeling. If possible, it would be great to have the same panel again next year. I like working with Rita a lot. We've become friends, we gel.'

Much as he has done with the public, in fact.

DISCOGRAPHY

SINGLES

Chills and Fever (1964)
It's Not Unusual (February 1965)
Once Upon a Time (March 1965)
Little Lonely One (May 1965 –
  produced by Joe Meek)
With These Hands (July 1965)
What's New Pussycat? (August 1965)
Lonely Joe (October 1965 –
  produced by Joe Meek)
Thunderball (January 1966)
To Make a Big Man Cry(1966)
Once There Was a Time/Not Responsible
  (May 1966)
This and That (August 1966)
The Green, Green Grass of Home
  (November 1966)
Detroit City (February 1967)
Funny, Familiar, Forgotten Feelings (April 1967)
I'll Never Fall In Love Again (July 1967)
I'm Coming Home (November 1967)
Delilah (February 1968)
Help Yourself (July 1968)
A Minute of Your Time (November 1968)
Love Me Tonight (May 1969)
Without Love (December 1969)
Daughter of Darkness (April 1970)

I (Who Have Nothing) (August 1970)
She's a Lady (January 1971)
My Way (1971)
Puppet Man (May 1971)
Till (October 1971)
The Young New Mexican Puppeteer
  (March 1972)
Golden Days (1973)
Letter to Lucille (April 1973)
Today I Started Loving You Again (1973)
La La La (1973)
Somethin' 'Bout You Baby I Like
  (September 1974)
Ain't No Love (1975)
I Got Your Number (1975)
Memories Don't Leave But People Do (1975)
Baby As You Turn Away (1976)
Say You'll Stay Until Tomorrow (April 1977)
No One Gave Me Love (1977)
Have You Ever Been Lonely? (1977)
Do You Take This Man (1979)
Darlin' (1981)
Love Is on the Radio (1984)
I'm an Old Rock 'N' Roller (1985)
A Boy from Nowhere (April 1987)
I Was Born To Be Me (December 1987)
Kiss (a cover of Prince's song with
  The Art of Noise) (October 1988)
Move Closer (April 1989)
Couldn't Say Goodbye (January 1991)
Carrying a Torch (with Van Morrison)
  (March 1991)
All You Need Is Love (February 1993)
If I Only Knew (October 1994)

Situation (1994)

I Wanna Get Back With You (with Tori Amos)
(March 1995)

You Can Leave Your Hat On (October 1997)

Burning Down the House (with The Cardigans)
(September 1999)

Baby, It's Cold Outside (with Cerys Matthews of
Catatonia) (December 1999)

Mama Told Me Not To Come
(with Stereophonics) (March 2000)

Sex Bomb (with Mousse T) (May 2000)

You Need Love Like I Do (Don't You)
(with Heather Small of M People,
cover of a Gladys Knight & the Pips song)
(November 2000)

Tom Jones International (October 2002)

Black Betty (February 2003)

It'll Be Me (with Jools Holland)
(September 2004)

Hold On I'm Coming (with John Farnham)
(2005)

Stoned in Love (with Chicane) (April 2006)

Cry for Home (with Van Morrison) (June 2007)

Islands in the Stream (March 2009)

Evil/Jezebel(with Jack White) (March 2012)

I'll Sail My Ship Alone (with Jools Holland)
(December 2012)

On My Own (with Robbie Williams)
(December 2012)

STUDIO ALBUMS

Along Came Jones (1965)

A-Tom-ic Jones (1966)
From the Heart (1966)
Green, Green Grass of Home (1967)
Delilah (1968)
Help Yourself (1968)
This Is Tom Jones (1969)
Tom (1970)
I Who Have Nothing (1970)
She's a Lady (1971)
Tom Jones Live at Caesar's Palace (1971)
Close Up (1972)
Somethin' 'Bout You Baby I Like (1974)
Memories Don't Leave Like People Do (1975)
Say You'll Stay Until Tomorrow (1977)
Darlin' (1981)
Don't Let Our Dreams Die Young (1983)
Move Closer (1988)
Carrying a Torch (1991)
The Lead and How to Swing It (1994)
From The Vaults (1998)
Reload (1999)
Mr Jones (2002)
Tom Jones and Jools Holland (2004)
Together In Concert (with John Farnham)
   (Australia, 2005)
24 Hours (2008)
Praise & Blame (2010)
Spirit in the Room (2012)

COMPILATION ALBUMS

13 Smash Hits (1967)
Tom Jones: Greatest Hits (1973)

Tom Jones: 20 Greatest Hits (1975)
Tom Jones Sings 24 Great Standards (1976)
What A Night (1978)
I'm Coming Home (1978)
Super Disc of Tom Jones (1979)
Tom Jones Sings The Hits (1979)
Do You Take This Man? (1979)
The Very Best of Tom Jones (1980)
Rescue Me (1980)
The Golden Hits (1980)
16 Love Songs (1983)
The Tom Jones Album (1983)
The Country Side of Tom Jones (1985)
The Soul of Tom Jones (1986)
Love Songs (1986)
The Great Love Songs (1987)
Tom Jones – The Greatest Hits (1987)
It's Not Unusual – His Greatest Hits (1987)
*The Legendary Tom Jones –
   30th Anniversary Album* (1995)
The Best of Tom Jones (1997)
The Ultimate Hits Collection (1998)
*From Las Vegas to London:
   the Best of Tom Jones Live* (1999)
The Best of Tom Jones (2001)
Greatest Hits (2003)
Duets (2003)
The Definitive: 1964-2002 (box set) (2003)
When I Fall in Love: 20 All-Time Classics
   (2005)
After Dark: Love Songs (2005)
Gold (2005)
54 Classic Hits (2005)
Greatest Hits: the Platinum Edition (2006)

The Hits (2006)
The Signature Collection: Tom Jones (2007)
Greatest Hits – Rediscovered (2010)

VIDEOS AND DVDS

Tom Jones Born To Be Me (1987)
Tom Jones Live at this Moment (1989)
This is Tom Jones (1992)
  (Programme content 1969–71)
This is Tom Jones Too (1993)
  (Programme content 1969–71)
Tom Jones One Night Only... (1996)
An Audience with Tom Jones (1999)
Tom Jones London Bridge Special (1999)
  (Programme content from 1974)
Tom Jones Classic Country (1999)
  (Programme content from 1980–81)
Tom Jones 35 Classic Ballads (2000)
  (Programme content from 1980–81)
Tom Jones – The Ultimate Collection
  (Programme content from 1980–81)
Tom Jones – Sincerely Yours (2002)
  (Programme
  content from 1980–81)
Tom Jones Live At Cardiff Castle (2002)
Tom Jones – Duets By Invitation Only (2002)
  (Programme content from 1980–81)
Tom Jones – Classic R & B and Funk (2004)
  (Programme content from 1980–81)
John Farnham & Tom Jones Together in Concert
  (2005)
Tom Jones Sounds in Motion LEGENDS IN

CONCERT (2006)
This is Tom Jones (2007)
Tom Jones Christmas (2007)
This is Tom Jones Volume 2: Legendary Performers
  (2008)
This is Tom Jones Volume 3: What's New Pussycat?
  (2009)

FILMOGRAPHY

Hex (1973)
Silk n' Sabotage (1994)
The Jerky Boys (1995)
Mars Attacks! (1996)
Agnes Browne (1999)

AWARDS AND ACHIEVEMENTS

1965: Grammy award for 'Best New Artist'
1967: 'World's Number One Vocalist'
  in US Disc Jockey Poll
1967: Broke all time box-office records at
  London's premier show places
  the Talk of Town and the Palladium theatre
1969: 'Showbiz Personality of the Year' by the
  Variety Club of Great Britain
1969: 'Top TV Personality of the Year'
1969: 'Top Male Singer'
1969: 'Top TV Artist'
1970: 'Entertainer of the Year' by
  America's Friars Club organisation
  of top showbusiness people

1970: Shattered the Madison Square Garden box office record in New York

1972: Voted World's Sexiest Male by readers of a women's magazine

1992: Asked to participate in The World Choir at Cardiff Arms Park

1999: Awarded an OBE in the New Year's honours list

2000: Brit award for 'Best British Male Vocalist'

2000: Bambi Award (an annual televison and media prize awarded by the German television magazine *Bild und Funk*) for comeback of the year

2003: Brit award for Outstanding Contribution to Music

2003: Lifetime Achievement Award for Outstanding Contribution to Music at the World Music Awards in Monaco

2006: Awarded a knighthood for his services to music in Queen Elizabeth II's annual New Year's honours list.

This Large Print Book for the partially sighted, who cannot read normal print, is published under the auspices of

THE ULVERSCROFT FOUNDATION

THE ULVERSCROFT FOUNDATION

... we hope that you have enjoyed this Large Print Book. Please think for a moment about those people who have worse eyesight problems than you ... and are unable to even read or enjoy Large Print, without great difficulty.

You can help them by sending a donation, large or small to:

**The Ulverscroft Foundation,
1, The Green, Bradgate Road,
Anstey, Leicestershire, LE7 7FU,
England.**
or request a copy of our brochure for more details.

The Foundation will use all your help to assist those people who are handicapped by various sight problems and need special attention.

Thank you very much for your help.